HAL

NURSING THROUGH SHOT AND SHELL

NURSING THROUGH SHOT AND SHELL

A Great War Nurse's Story

Edited and with an Introduction
by Dr Vivien Newman

Pen & Sword
MILITARY

First published in Great Britain in 2014 by
PEN AND SWORD MILITARY
an imprint of
Pen and Sword Books Ltd
47 Church Street
Barnsley
South Yorkshire S70 2AS

Copyright © Dr Vivien Newman and Christine Smyth

ISBN 978 1 47382 759 2

The right of Dr Vivien Newman and Christine Smyth
to be identified as the authors of this work has been asserted by them
in accordance with the Copyright, Designs and Patents Act 1988.

Printed and bound in England
by CPI Group (UK) Ltd, Croydon, CR0 4YY

Typeset in Times by CHIC GRAPHICS

Pen & Sword Books Ltd incorporates the imprints of Pen & Sword
Archaeology, Atlas, Aviation, Battleground, Discovery, Family
History, History, Maritime, Military, Naval, Politics, Railways,
Select, Social History, Transport, True Crime, Claymore Press,
Frontline Books, Leo Cooper, Praetorian Press, Remember When,
Seaforth Publishing and Wharncliffe.

For a complete list of Pen and Sword titles please contact
Pen and Sword Books Limited
47 Church Street, Barnsley, South Yorkshire, S70 2AS, England
E-mail: enquiries@pen-and-sword.co.uk
Website: www.pen-and-sword.co.uk

Contents

—w—

Dedication

—⟋⟍—

For my surgeon grandfather, Major Arthur Scott Turner, RAMC, FRCS, who served in St Omer 1916–1919. He and Beatrice may well have met.

Dr Vivien Newman

I would like to dedicate this book to Beatrice's two granddaughters, Heidi and Molly.

To Heidi for coming to track down her English relatives all those years ago and to Molly for realising the importance of the diary and saving it for us all to enjoy.

Christine Smyth

Abbreviations

—⁓—

ADMS	Assistant Director Medical Services
ARRC	Associate Royal Red Cross
BEF	British Expeditionary Force
BJN	*British Journal of Nursing*
CAMC	Canadian Army Medical Corps
CCS	Casualty Clearing Station
DDMS	Deputy Director Medical Services
DGMS	Director General Medical Services
GH	General Hospital
MM	Military Medal
MO	Medical Officer
NGH	Northern General Hospital
QAIMNS	Queen Alexandra Imperial Military Nursing Service
QAIMNS(R)	Queen Alexandra Imperial Military Nursing Service (Reserve)
QANNS	Queen Alexandra Naval Nursing Service
QANNS(R)	Queen Alexandra Naval Nursing Service (Reserve)
RAMC	Royal Army Medical Service
RRC	Royal Red Cross
RTO	Railway Transport Officer
SIW	Self-Inflicted Wound
TFNS	Territorial Forces Nursing Service
USANC	United States Army Nurse Corps
VAD	Voluntary Aid Detachment
VC	Victoria Cross
YMCA	Young Men's Christian Association
YWCA	Young Women's Christian Association

Acknowledgements

—ळ—

My greatest thanks are to Beatrice Hopkinson, her descendants and family members. I hope they feel the pages that follow honour the service and the memory of a truly inspirational woman. She is amongst the finest of the unsung heroines of the Great War. Like so many professional nurses, she never sought the limelight but uncomplainingly, modestly and steadfastly remained at her post throughout some of the worst years of the war.

My husband Ivan entered enthusiastically and willingly into the history of World War One nursing, Casualty Clearing Stations, and St Omer, reading multiple drafts and, as always, playing Devil's Advocate (in the nicest possible way!). Throughout the writing of this project, he has been my sternest critic and my greatest fan. His admiration for Beatrice now rivals my own.

Battlefield guide and military historian Keith Dolan rose to the challenge of compressing Operations Michael and Georgette into little more than 500 words. His skill at making the most complex aspects of First World War history comprehensible to a non-specialist audience is only surpassed by his ability to guide pilgrims round the battlefields and cemeteries of the Western Front and Gallipoli. You can contact him by email, via keith.dolan@gmail.com either to 'Follow in the Steps of Beatrice Hopkinson' or to request a tailor-made tour.

Sarah Rogers refused to be defeated by the paucity of available information about 20 CCS. I am truly grateful for her perseverance in revealing Mary Bayne Lawson as the final missing name in the cast of characters within Beatrice's memoir.

The Head of Collections at Lincoln County Library most generously agreed to an Interlibrary Loan for *The Magazine: the Monthly Record of the 4th Northern General Hospital*. Clare Russell joined me in some photographic detective work.

Commissioning Editor Jen Newby, formerly of Pen & Sword Books, may not have realised what a remarkable journey she was sending me on when she wondered if I would 'have a look' at Beatrice's diary. I am very grateful to her for this request and for her leniency when I invariably exceeded the agreed word count.

Dr Vivien Newman, 2014

Foreword

—∿—

A Heroine in the Family

In 1979 I discovered that our family had American relatives. I was 24 years old and just married. I was visiting my mother when she told me that her cousin's daughter, Heidi, would be travelling to England from Puyallup, Washington, a small town in the hills above Seattle. This was the first time any of our American relatives had contacted us.

I was intrigued. We had family in America! Why had no one mentioned them before now? Who were they? How old was Heidi? So many questions came into my head.

My mother then told me a story which has stayed with me all these years and which I now feel, on the imminent centenary of the Great War, should be told. Beatrice Hopkinson was my mother's aunt. As a nursing sister, at the age of 27, she left England and her family to serve in the Great War of 1914–1918. There she met her future husband, Dr Charles Aylen. After the war he sent for her to join him in Canada, where they were married.

With only the tickets Charles had sent to her for the sea passage to Canada and the train journey to meet him in Winnipeg, Beatrice departed on a voyage into the unknown. Leaving her family and not knowing when she would see them again, but with love in her heart, she set off on a journey of a lifetime.

Over the years we have remained in touch with our American relatives. However, it was only recently that I learned of a diary Beatrice had written, detailing her time in France during the war. This diary is not only a historical record of the Great War, but a truly emotional story, giving us an insight into the conditions these brave people suffered for our freedom.

Christine Smyth (Beatrice Hopkinson's great-niece),
Dorset, England, 2013

Introduction

—ᘉᘉ—

The Publication of the Diary

As I was finishing a book about women in the First World War, the publishers, Pen & Sword, asked me to read a wartime memoir sent in by a nurse's descendants. They felt that this fascinating account needed editing to make it more accessible to a wider audience.

I awaited the typescript's arrival with some scepticism, however. Perhaps this was one more nursing tale that was jumping on the 1914–1918 Centenary bandwagon. Was the memoirist a professional nurse or was she a VAD? Whilst being an understandably precious document for her family, was this war diary in any way special? Indeed, had she even been 'at the Front' – or as close to the Front as women were allowed to get? I would keep an open mind.

The document arrived, and I immediately realised that this was indeed a remarkable account. Beatrice Hopkinson, by her own admission, did not possess any great 'literary talent' but the story that she had to tell far outweighed any shortcomings in the writing – this memoir truly extends our understanding of Great War nursing.

Beatrice was not a military nurse, nor a veteran of the Boer War; she was not a member of the carefully selected Queen Alexandra's Imperial Military Nursing Service; she was not a graduate of one of the great London Teaching Hospitals; she was definitely not a socially privileged VAD. She had merely trained in a Nottingham fever hospital and quietly risen to heights of professionalism and skill which, in a less tumultuous era, she may never have known she possessed. Nevertheless, Beatrice became one of an elite group of nurses who formed what we would now call 'rapid response' teams. Selected for their stamina and skill, as well as their level-headedness, these six-person teams worked during some of the harshest times in some of the most challenging nursing environments: the Casualty Clearing Stations (CCS) of the Western Front. This 'teamwork' was an aspect of Great War nursing that I, and I suspect many World War One historians, knew nothing about.

Despite its revelatory content, the memoir nevertheless posed challenges. All forms of writing are mediated, diaries and memoirs no less so. Some are governed by the story the diarist wants to tell about themselves or, when considering diaries kept during a war, the realisation that the diary may contribute to 'History'. Others are just written for the diarist, however much historians may pick over them when re-constructing lives. Beatrice's work fits into the latter category of 'writing for self'.

There are things Beatrice would have deliberately chosen to include in her diary, others she may have excluded for multiple reasons, including prosaic ones: after spending hours on her feet, nursing under the most difficult of conditions, she may often have been too tired, perhaps even too down-hearted, to scrawl more than a few words on the page. At times she would not have had the energy to write anything at all.

During the most frenetic times, nurses in CCS, and indeed all military hospitals, grabbed a few hours' rest – 'sleep' is too strong a word for the activity – sometimes just on stretchers on the ground. Even when there were a few spare moments, a writer needs, in Virginia Woolf's words, 'A room of one's own'. There were many times when Beatrice would not have had the luxury of a bed, let alone a room where she could place her writing materials and complete her diary entries.

On other occasions, an event may have seemed unimportant and not worth noting down, including, frustratingly at times, the location or even the identifying number of the CCS to which she was posted. Some happenings may have been so momentous that she felt she would never forget them – although with the passing of time, she might have done so. Others may have simply not interested her. And, above all, she was modest – there is nothing to indicate that she thought what she was doing was in any way exceptional.

Whilst trying to resolve some of these challenges, it was equally essential to retain Beatrice's voice. Yet, the memoir had to be comprehensible to readers with little specialist knowledge about First World War nursing and the way the Army Nursing Services developed. Clarity was needed for readers who were unsure about the differences between the amateur VAD nurses and the professionals, let alone the various Military Nursing Corps, and for those unfamiliar with exactly how the military action was unfolding on the Western Front between July 1917, when Beatrice arrived, until after the Armistice. Above all it had to be accessible for any readers or researchers who were interested in nursing services during the war.

After several abortive attempts at interspersing Beatrice's own memoir with editorial comments (these are now kept to a minimum of explanatory notes), I decided to divide the book into two distinct sections. The first would explain the background of both army and civilian nursing from the end of the nineteenth century to 1911–12, when Beatrice began training as a fever nurse. The narrative would edge closer to Beatrice herself, her family, her culture, until the point when, in 1914, she began nursing military patients at Lincoln County Hospital, the 4th Northern General Hospital, Lincoln.

Guiding readers through the First Aid, hospital and patient evacuation services, both at the Front and in Britain, seemed essential, as did transporting readers into war-torn France (and subsequently Belgium), where Beatrice arrived in 1917. She was a novice on arrival but the war was then entering one of its most bitter phases; she would have to learn the ropes and learn them fast.

One thing still seemed lacking in all the information that I was accumulating. I am by training and by instinct a social historian and no historical individual functions in a vacuum. But, following the more reticent mores of the time, apart from her sisters Gertrude and Doris who are named once, and her 'Boy', Charles Aylen, Beatrice mentions nobody else by their full name. To flesh out her world I needed to try to find at least some of the people with whom she came into contact. A few became identifiable, they too had interesting tales to tell which increase our understanding of Beatrice and the world she operated in and, at times, against. Others refused to emerge from the shadows; I have given names and additional information about them where these details have been traced. Both those I found and some of those who remain hidden would have played a part in turning Beatrice into the exceptional nurse she became. They would have influenced her, just as she would have influenced them.

This memoir is therefore not just one more nurse's wartime diary. It contributes to the important, but still under-researched historiography of the professional nurses of the First World War, those who would never have anticipated becoming military nurses but who, when their country called, willingly, if quietly, answered. Those who, in the words of the wartime 'Agreement' they signed when they were enrolled in the Territorial Forces Nursing Service, pledged, 'to devote my whole time and professional skills to my service'. None could have done this more wholeheartedly, professionally and uncomplainingly than Beatrice.

The first section of the book is thus the background and the cast of players, with a brief 'Military Interlude', while the second consists of Beatrice's own account of nursing through shot and shell. I hope you gain as much pleasure from reading the memoir as I have had from preparing it for publication.

Dr Vivien Newman, 2014

I

The Historial Background to Beatrice Hopkinson's Diary

by Dr Vivien Newman

—⚡—

Army Nursing: 'Jobs for the Ladies'

During the First World War, the women of the Voluntary Aid Detachments (VADs) captured – and indeed still capture – the public imagination. Dubbed the 'Roses of No-Man's Land', lauded by the contemporary press and immortalised in memoirs, fiction and on the small screen, these generally well-born young women have incorrectly become synonymous with the Nursing Services of the First World War.

Their commitment and dedication is beyond question and many paid with their lives for their service to the British Army. However, they were nursing auxiliaries and the professional nurses of the permanent Queen Alexandra's Imperial Nursing Service (QAIMNS), the Queen Alexandra's Royal Naval Nursing Service (QARNNS), their Reserves, and the Territorial Forces Nursing Service (TFNS), were the backbone of the military and naval nursing services.

Since the days of 'The Lady with the Lamp' and long before, albeit unofficially, Britain has called upon her women during times of war. But it was in 1860, six years after the Crimean War ended, that women first entered military hospitals. Florence Nightingale's endeavours to create a body of military nurses had borne fruit and the Army Training School for Military Nurses was established at the Royal Victoria Hospital in Netley, Southampton. It would be another 20 years before the Army Nursing

Service (ANS) was formed. This embryonic service's stringent code of regulations was rigidly attentive to aspiring recruits' social background. Aged between 25 and 35, they should be of high social status, and ideally daughters or widows of army officers. According to the then Surgeon-General, Sir William Hooper, this 'entail[*ed*] a good social qualification'.

In 1882, with Florence Nightingale's order, 'your every word and act [*should*] be worthy of your profession and your womanhood,' ringing in their ears, a small, carefully chosen group of nurses from the fledgling ANS accompanied the British Army overseas, bound for the now long-forgotten Egyptian Campaign. They beat a path that thousands of army nurses, including Beatrice Hopkinson, have since trodden with dedication, distinction and scant regard for personal safety.

If this 1882 campaign and those of the following 17 years made little impression upon most civilians, then arrangements for the nursing of soldiers made even less. Few civilians would have read the May 1890 *Illustrated Naval and Military Magazine* article about 'Her Majesty's Nursing Sisters', which disclosed that there were a total of 60 army nurses working in 16 military hospitals in the United Kingdom and overseas.

It was the Second Boer War (1899–1902) which revolutionised both army nursing and public interest therein. In 1899, the one Lady Superintendent, 19 superintendents (senior nursing sisters), 68 sisters and the 100 members of the Army Nursing Service and Army Nursing Reserve (all of impeccable social status), found themselves tasked with caring for the largest army Britain had ever sent into combat overseas. As would happen 15 years later, these initial numbers were soon found to be woefully inadequate.

Eventually, 22 general hospitals were opened in South Africa, each staffed by about 20 nurses. Attired in a suitably adapted uniform, including 'canvas gaiters as protection against snakes', these so-called 'gentlewomen' soon discovered, in the words of Georgina Pope of the Canadian Nursing Reserve, that, 'We too were soldiers.' Georgina nursed both in the 'huts at Wynburg and under canvas at Rondebosch' where, at times, she made what she considered 'a too intimate acquaintance with scorpions and snakes.' In South Africa, nurses experienced conditions that would become familiar to women who served in Britain's next conflict. Writing in the *British Journal of Nursing*, Georgina Pope explained that, 'Hanging in our mess was a copy of orders to be observed when attacked, &c. Several mornings we wakened to hear the boom of guns.'

Some of the nurses in this opening war of the twentieth century were trapped in the infamous Siege of Kimberley, where they treated Boer prisoners as well as their own wounded and sick. Others were at Ladysmith, where General White singled out for praise the nurses who 'maintained throughout the siege a brave and protracted struggle against sickness under almost every possible disadvantage, their numbers being most inadequate for the work to be done.'

There were nurses too at Mafeking, whose relief was greeted with national jubilation. In his Mafeking Dispatch, Lord Roberts specifically mentioned the army nurses who 'worked with the greatest zeal and self devotion throughout the siege.' He drew attention to the 'heavy work, frequently carried out under fire … It was largely due to their unremitting devotion and skill that the wounded, in so many cases, made marvellous recoveries, and the health of the garrison remained so good.'

Army nurses also shared many of the hardships of the troops they had gone overseas to nurse. In one of the most remote outposts, Captain William Dobbin saw Australian nurses:

on their knees scrubbing and cleaning ... to receive the patients, and in the middle of their work 10 or 12 sick and dying men dumped down from an ox wagon – no orderlies detailed, no native servants. The nurses would be obliged to take off some of their own clothing to make pillows for the sick men, and then go outside to cook food under a raging sun.

What is as noticeable in the writings of these South African War nurses, as in First World War nurses' accounts, is their admiration for their patients. 'The arrival of this convoy was the most pitiful sight,' wrote Georgina Pope, 'many of the men being stretcher cases shot through thigh, foot or spine. What struck one most was the wonderful pluck of these poor fellows who had jolted over the rough veldt in ambulances and then endured the long train journey.'

As they would do in the 1914-18 war, nurses also shared the highs and lows of their daily activities in their letters home. Writing to her sister Rosie from 'this Godforsaken country' at 11.00pm on Good Friday, 28 March 1902, Kate Luard (who returned to service in 1914, once again writing prolific letters) explained how she had 'been on the trot' since 8.00am. She recounted that, 'The wards are awful busy again – at least mine are – & on Easter Day we get the Klerksdorp wounded & shall have a high old time.' Three hours off-duty where, astride her horse Ginger, Kate 'jump[*ed*] the trench, and then [*went*] bucketing over the veldt to the tops of Angel Kopjes with heaven born views and Transvaal colours,' left her ready to cope with her patients and her 'deaf and worried orderly', even though both patients and orderly were 'rather trying tonight'. Although some off-duty time was located where possible on a daily basis, it appears that after a year's service nurses got ten days' leave, which they frequently spent in Natal.

Although nursing duties form the bulk of the writings of both the South African and First World War nurses, women from both conflicts also found time to comment on the food they resorted to eating. One nurse was unimpressed by 'Trek Ox' which 'was so tough that it is difficult to tackle'. At Ladysmith, although Kate Driver was happy to eat horse, she 'cannot say the same for the 'cow-heel jelly made from the horse hoof which was occasionally available to us nurses. It was most sickly, and often by the time it reached our hospital, it was fermenting. It was dyed mauve – as an encouragement I suppose.' Georgina Pope found that although fresh milk was non-existent, 'condensed milk, beef-tea, and champagne' were plentiful.

Georgina Pope's summing up of her experiences in South Africa could have been penned by a Great War nurse: 'I deemed it a great privilege to aid in caring for the sick and wounded, and while the hardships necessarily endured in such a campaign have faded from my mind, I still often seem to hear the "Thank you, sister," of the grateful soldier.'

Unlike Britain's other late nineteenth century wars, this conflict did impact upon the national consciousness, as stories, both of the wounded and of the nursing service, gained wide press coverage. Just under 40 nurses (including one Australian) died of disease; Rudyard Kipling praised the women's sacrifice, imagining their 'little wasted bodies, ah, so light to lower down' into their graves. The dubious honour of being the first woman whose name is engraved on a war memorial (in St Helen's, Lancashire), fell to Army Nursing Reserve Sister Clara Evans. She is named alongside local men who also 'Died On Active Service' in South Africa. Sister Dorlinda Bessie Hyland, another of the 47 nurses who died during the campaign, is also mentioned on a plaque in the Trinity Reformed Church, Lancaster.

A number of the veteran nurses of this conflict returned to the fray a decade later. Perhaps, like old soldiers, they helped to steady the nerves of the younger nurses working close to the guns for the first time. As we shall see in Beatrice's diary, nurses could find themselves calmly performing their duties as battle raged close by. Yet, even old South Africa hands would be horrified by the new types of injuries and wounds they were called upon to deal with. South Africa veteran Kate Luard was not alone in feeling that the 'wounds of the Boer War were pin-pricks' compared to what nursing personnel now faced. The most famous of the South Africa nursing veterans was Dame Maud McCarthy who, by 1910, was principal matron at the War Office. McCarthy arrived in France to take up her post as Matron-in-Chief to the BEF in August 1914.

By the time the very first army nurses embarked from Folkestone on 15 August 1914, the Service to which they belonged had been significantly re-organised. A Royal Warrant of 27 March 1902 had brought the Queen Alexandra's Imperial Military Nursing Service (QAIMNS) into being. Over a decade later, the social status and educational background of aspiring recruits to this new service remained paramount. 'Profession or Occupation of Father' was the question asked immediately after name, date and place of birth on the initial application form. 'Unsatisfactory social status' could still lead, even during the Great War, to a nurse's application being rejected, irrespective of her professional skills.

Perhaps unsurprisingly, the QAIMNS had struggled to find enough recruits of suitable background and in August 1914 it was under strength. A total of 297 QAIMNS members – matrons, sisters and staff nurses – were employed in military hospitals at home and overseas. During the Great War these numbers remained unchanged. It was considered unwise to permanently employ more women than would be needed when hostilities ceased. Women who resigned were replaced, but the many thousands of nurses who were recruited to the Army Nursing Services during the war were on short-term contracts ('as long as my services are required'), with clauses enabling the War Office to terminate their employment at its convenience.

In 1908, the Territorial Forces and the Territorial Forces Nursing Service (TFNS) had been formed specifically for Home, as opposed to Overseas, Service. The social requirements for this new nursing service were less stringent and no mention was made of background, although professional requirements were high. Candidates had to be over the age of 23 and have already completed three years' training in a recognised hospital – these did not include fever, or women and children's hospitals, although this rule was relaxed in August 1915. These nurses remained civilians; they received no additional pay; and had to confirm their commitment to the TFNS on an annual basis.

Apart from the Territorial matrons, who spent a week training in military hospitals every two years, no additional military nursing training was considered necessary. Like the QAIMNS, TFNS members mobilised immediately when war was declared, probably only anticipating serving in military hospitals at home. Few would have guessed that between 1914 and 1918, of the 8,140 nurses who enrolled in the Service during hostilities, 2,280 would serve overseas. Forty-eight gave their lives, including six who were killed by enemy action, not to mention those who later suffered debilitating mental after-effects, as one of Beatrice Hopkinson's overseas matrons would do. Reading Beatrice's memoir, it seems surprising that the numbers of fatalities were not higher.

During the decade when the Army Nursing Service was being transformed, civilian nursing was also undergoing its own travails. In 1905 a Select Committee had reported in favour of State Registration of nurses – hitherto the profession had been largely unregulated. Doyenne of British nursing Florence Nightingale was amongst the anti-regulation voices. She believed nursing was a vocation that could not and should not be 'taught, examined or regulated'. The dispute rumbled on, the final Bill leading to State Registration only being passed by Parliament in 1919.

In 1908, the foundation of a Fever Nurses' Association had led to a scheme of fever training. The *British Journal of Nursing* (*BJN*) hoped and believed that this would lead to an improvement both in the training and the status of fever nurses, with the end result being 'an increase in the popularity' of fever nursing, as well as crucially, 'enhancing the status' of nurses working in fever hospitals. The subtext here appears to be that those trained in such hospitals were deemed of lower status than those who had trained in the main teaching hospitals from where the QAIMNS were predominantly drawn. Nursing was far from immune to the contemporary angst about social status.

Beatrice Hopkinson: From Chambermaid to Nurse
It is unlikely that the early travails and formation of the various military

nursing services between 1880 and 1908 would have been known, or indeed of interest, to the Hopkinson family. That Beatrice herself would become a military nurse who not only served with the British Army overseas but also nursed under enemy fire, would have seemed unimaginable during her childhood.

Like their coal miner, shoe-maker and carter neighbours, George and his wife Damaris were undoubtedly more concerned with the everyday demands and needs of their rapidly increasing family than with the welfare of soldiers fighting in distant campaigns. By 1901 George had risen from the position of grocer's assistant to a grocer's manager, but in 1900 tragedy had struck the family, bringing Beatrice's childhood to an abrupt end at the tender age of 11.

Thirty-five-year-old Damaris had died whilst carrying her seventh child and with four younger siblings, Beatrice and her elder sister Gertrude would have found themselves shouldering many of the responsibilities that, in happier circumstances, would have been their mother's. An ability to both care for others and cope calmly with whatever hardships and dangers came her way appears to have been a hallmark of Beatrice's war service.

In 1908, George re-married. The 1911 census reveals that he and his youngest daughter were residing with his in-laws near Sheffield. Damaris' other children were dispersed; the census reveals that 15-year-old Edith was a kitchen maid in Sheffield, while joiner Charles and plumber's apprentice Wilfred were living separately in Rotherham, and Beatrice was a chambermaid at the Portland Hall Hotel in Mansfield, Nottinghamshire. It is tempting to think that she may have had some conversation with one Portland Hall Hotel boarder, who was an RAMC recruiting officer, and this may have fired her interest in army nursing.

Nothing in Beatrice's memoir explains what led her into nursing. She simply writes that she began her training in 1910 at the Fever Hospital in Nottingham. However, her memory has proved slightly faulty. Not only did the 1911 census place her at the Mansfield hotel, but the Nottingham General Hospital Fever Wards were only created in 1911, largely through the munificence of local mine owner and benefactor Sir Charles Seely.

Outside London, fever hospitals were frequently founded, funded and independently operated by local authorities. Sir Charles may have been prompted to create this new facility as, between 1895 and 1900,

Nottingham's average yearly incidence of cholera and enteric fever was 489 cases (possibly slightly above the national average), with 73 deaths. It was through fever nursing, however, that Beatrice took the initial steps that would lead her first to war and, eventually, across the Atlantic to an unknown future in late 1919.

Margaret Currie, in *Fever Hospitals and Fever Nurses* (2004), argues that fever nurses were under-appreciated, exploited and even suffered 'ghettoization'. From age 17, women could start their arduous training, fixed at a minimum period of two years for untrained nurses. According to surviving records at Glasgow University Schools of Medicine, fever nurses spent an average of 14 hours out of every 24 on duty, with one afternoon off every fortnight. Documentary evidence indicates that probationers were on the wards from almost the minute they arrived at the hospital; learning was predominantly 'on the job', with instruction squeezed into their few precious off-duty hours. Dorothy Moriarty, who trained as a nurse during the war, remembered how 'we were pushed into a ward without any preliminary teaching.'

Along with the gruelling schedule, the need for 'quickness, quietness, method and observation' was stressed. However, 'rough domestic chores' were excluded from their duties. This would have been one bonus for Beatrice who, as first a surrogate mother and later a hotel chambermaid, must have had enough of 'rough domestic chores.' It is probable that she became a fever nurse as this was the more accessible entrée into the nursing profession for a young woman of almost certainly very limited financial means, as the main teaching hospitals often required fee payment from nursing probationers.

Although some of the skills considered vital for peace-time fever nursing would be irrelevant for front line war nursing, rigorous adherence to others, including 'precautions against self-infection', could, quite literally, save nurses' as well as patients' lives. In the chaotic and highly septic conditions of Great War nursing, where patients suffered extensively from sickness and septicaemia in addition to wounds, the 'exemplary hygiene' stressed by Matron Violetta Thurstan MM in her 1917 *Text Book of War Nursing*, was paramount. More than one nurse died from sepsis and many were hospitalised, so nurses were always alert to its first signs in their patients.

Having completed her fever training some time in 1913, Beatrice moved to the County Hospital Lincoln as a probationer. Many hospitals still considered training on the job more important than theoretical classroom knowledge. Drudgery was almost a *sine qua non* of probationers' lives. They were at the beck and call of staff nurses, sisters and, should they cross their paths, matrons. 'Rough domestic chores' may well have been back on the agenda, for probationers' duties included much 'sweeping, dusting and polishing', although how many of these tasks would have fallen to the fever-trained Beatrice is impossible to know.

If she had time to stop and contemplate the future, she assuredly saw herself working her way up the hierarchical nursing ladder; perhaps her ambitions stretched to progressing to sister or even the pinnacle of nursing: matron.

From Fever Nurse to Wartime Army Nurse: 'Our Poor Boys'

Whatever ambitions Beatrice cherished for the future were forever altered on 28 June 1914. The heir to the Austro-Hungarian Empire was shot and fatally wounded, plunging Europe into a war that would place the greatest of strains not only on the Armed Forces but also every facet of the publicly and privately funded medical services. Beatrice would, inevitably, be swept up in the turmoil when, on 4 August 1914, Britain entered the Great European War.

Like many civilian hospitals the length and breadth of the land, the County Hospital Lincoln was soon on a wartime footing. Beatrice notes how three wards were commandeered by the War Office and, almost by default, she found herself caring for wounded soldiers. The first convoy of 105 patients reached the hospital on 13 September 1914, news of its imminent arrival having been received the day before. The following day, the hospital was showered with gifts from the local population, keen to show their appreciation to the wounded soldiers.

Nurses at home may initially have been unfamiliar with the stages that would bring those whom Beatrice called 'our poor boys' back to England or, indeed, what the medical facilities were like in France. As the war continued, by the time a soldier reached a hospital bed in England, he had already been through a lengthy process.

The true function of the Army Medical Services was to return a man to active service. At the heart of this lay the triage system. This ran counter to nurses' and medical professionals' instincts, as in this system of assessment the least seriously injured (and thus the most likely to survive and return to duty) took priority, whilst the most seriously wounded were attended to last – if at all. The horrors of the 'moribund' tents, where the dying were placed and left to die, traumatised many medical professionals.

A wounded man's first contact with the Medical Services was at the Regimental Aid Post, often situated in reserve trenches and very near the front line. Staffed by the Battalion Medical Officer (MO), male orderlies and stretcher bearers, here wounded soldiers received minimal medical care, often little more than a field dressing and perhaps a 'smoke' or a mug of Bovril. Those whose wounds were more than superficial or not yet fatal, were moved back, either on foot, carried by a member of their Unit, or by wheeled stretcher to (male staffed) Advanced Dressing Stations, where wounds were dressed and more basic treatment was provided. From here, those whose injuries were still considered sufficiently serious were moved to Casualty Clearing Stations (CCS). Beatrice would become intimately involved with the workings of these places.

CCS were, in the first three months of the war, male-only preserves. In late October 1914, Maud McCarthy, Matron-in-Chief to the British Expeditionary Force, had been asked to provide initially five nurses for each of the often overwhelmed CCS on the Western Front. Usually situated around 20 kilometres from the front line – itself a fluid construct – CCS were, at least in the early days, situated in buildings such as schools, factories and existing hospitals. As the war progressed and the need for facilities increased exponentially, tents or huts were erected to accommodate the ever-mounting casualties; some developed their own medical 'specialisms'.

CCS evolved into large, well-equipped, if impermanent, hospitals often placed close to railway sidings to facilitate the transport and transfer of the wounded. Such locations would make them particularly vulnerable to enemy fire, as Beatrice and countless other nurses discovered. As each CCS covered about half a mile of land, it is hardly surprising that many nurses talk of being rushed off their feet due to the large distances they had to cover, frequently, it seemed, in weather so inclement that they resorted to tucking their long skirts up or into their rubber boots.

Eventually numbering 72 in total, CCS were equipped to perform serious operations and although, ideally, wounded men would spend only a short time here, some remained for days or even weeks, due to the inherent dangers of moving them further back, either by Ambulance Train or Hospital Barge to Base Hospitals. The whole process was highly organised and extremely efficient. CCS were a focal point in respect to both treatment of wounds and prevention of disease. They were staffed exclusively by qualified professional nurses; contrary to popular myth, no VADs ever served there.

The QAIMNS/TFNS nurses were frequently hand-picked for this most arduous of nursing roles; skill, stamina and steadiness were essential requirements, all of which Beatrice had in abundance. Those who were not considered up to the particular challenges CCS posed were removed. The contribution of nurses such as Beatrice to the care of the wounded in these facilities cannot be over-estimated.

Stationary and General Hospitals were positioned much further behind the lines, at least until the lines moved and caught up with them. There is often confusion between these treatment areas. Stationary Hospitals, despite their name, were equipped for field work and could be easily moved. Accommodating up to 400 casualties, they were generally situated within civilian hospitals in larger towns or cities. General Hospitals (GH), like 59GH where Beatrice initially served overseas, were intended to be permanent. Being located near railway lines made it easier for them to receive casualties from CCS up the line and transport them onwards to England via sea ports – this also facilitated the arrival of staff from disembarkation ports.

Some General Hospitals were housed in large buildings such as hotels, casinos, sports stadia, prisons or even lunatic asylums, whilst others consisted of huts, tents or marquees erected on open ground. There are a number of references in Maud McCarthy's diaries to additional huts being constructed to increase capacity. There could often be a considerable distance between the facilities which came under the governance of one General Hospital. Eight kilometres separated the officers' wards of 59GH from the main hospital, putting additional strain on staffing arrangements. There was a higher nurse-to-patient ratio in officers' wards.

Base Hospitals represented the final stage of overseas military medical facilities. Situated near the army's principal bases, each was staffed by 32 medical officers, 3 chaplains, 73 nurses, significant numbers of volunteers (such as VADs), and 206 troops acting as orderlies, who took their orders from nurses and performed the most intimate nursing tasks, which it was not considered appropriate for women to undertake. Some orderlies rose heroically to the demands of the job, others resented being answerable to women, a situation with which they would have been entirely unfamiliar, resentful of and often uncomfortable about. Women occupying positions where they could give orders to men were almost unheard of at this time.

Soldiers who had made it this far back remained in the hospital until they recovered sufficiently to be returned to Active Service. The 'lucky' ones (about 40 per cent of total admissions to hospitals overseas), whose conditions were considered suitably critical, were given a 'Blighty Ticket', meaning that they would be transferred by hospital ship back to England. Patients' joy when the precious 'Blighty Ticket' came their way was often boundless. As May Bradford, who was dubbed the 'Letter Writer to the British Army', noted in her memoir, those who were well enough to do so, clutched their tickets in their hands, reluctant to be parted from them for a second.

Back in Blighty, there was a massive network of hospitals; some, like the Lincoln County Hospital, were official peace-time hospitals with wards commandeered by the army. Other hospitals were established in private mansions or in buildings with quite unrelated peace-time uses, taken over and turned into hospitals as facilities became ever more stretched. Forward planning in the years preceding the war ensured that the hospital services were ready to leap into action, although none could have foreseen the demands that would be placed upon them.

When the TFNS was formed, the country was divided into six regions and provision was made for 23 Territorial Force hospitals in towns and cities across the country, each able to accommodate 520 patients. (By the end of 1917 they had a total of 48,234 beds.) These hospitals were, in modern-day terms, 'virtual' hospitals which, on the outbreak of war would take over schools and other public buildings, requiring their owners to vacate them.

Each one would be staffed by 91 trained nurses, although 120 women were recruited for each hospital: 2 matrons, 30 sisters and 88 staff nurses. A recently published book (*Stories From The War Hospital*) about the 2nd Northern General Hospital (2NGH), where Mabel Whiffin, Beatrice's first matron in France and a number of Beatrice's first colleagues served, reveals how quickly a building could be transformed.

2NGH was housed in the City of Leeds Training College (now part of Leeds Metropolitan University), which opened in June 1913 – during the ceremony, a suffragette was thrown into the swimming-pool. Within a week of war being declared, 600 beds were available; the trainee teachers had moved out and the medical staff, including the Matron-in-Chief of the Leeds General Infirmary, moved in.

Although the hospitals on the Home Front were soon ready to receive their patients, the patients still needed to be transported to the hospitals. Conveying the wounded was initially problematic for, despite the fanfare which often greeted the boys at railway stations – frequently the Mayor in full regalia, with his chain of office around his neck, and other civic dignitaries would be on the platform and cheering crowds lining the streets – no official transport was laid on. Lincoln Hospital was not alone in hiring, as Beatrice remembered, 'traction' vans and furniture lorries, although intensive local fund-raising often meant that a town soon boasted its own fleet of ambulances. The most severely wounded or disfigured men would often be brought in at night – it was believed that seeing the most horrific injuries and disfigurements would lower public morale.

The 4th Northern General Hospital (4NGH) – where newly qualified Staff Nurse Beatrice Hopkinson took her first steps in military nursing – underwent a similar rapid transformation. Before the war, 4NGH was Lincoln Grammar School (now Lincoln Christ's Hospital School). The pupils were moved elsewhere, only returning in 1920. The October 1914 edition of the school's magazine, *The Lincolnian*, proudly announced that (at that point) the school was the only one in England to have been transformed into a hospital, with additional huts being erected in the playing fields. Archival data reveals that after its creation in August 1914, 4NGH treated over 45,000 men; 118 trained and 87 untrained personnel cared for 41 officers' and 1,126 other ranks' beds.

One photograph, almost certainly taken at Christmastime, shows a ward of double amputees; they would have passed through the hospital's dedicated amputation theatre, which Beatrice mentions in her memoirs. Many are in hospital 'Blues', the uniform worn by those well enough to spend at least part of the day out of bed; patients were first and foremost soldiers. In British hospitals, to the bemusement of many Australian nurses, these patients had to stand to attention at the foot of their bed when MOs and visiting dignitaries made their rounds. The legless were expected to 'sit to' attention.

At 4NGH, Beatrice would have nursed men who hailed from far and wide across the United Kingdom. If a British soldier was expected to be in hospital for more than three months attempts were generally made to transfer him to somewhere closer to his home, otherwise logistics of bed vacancies and, indeed, places on trains to transport him governed where he ended up. The exceptions were the Colonial soldiers who, wherever possible, were sent to their own facilities and were often nursed by their compatriots. On her arrival in London, Beatrice comments on the number of Colonial nurses she saw, who had flocked to the 'Mother Country'.

Beatrice was placed in the 'Heavy Surgical' Ward, where the most severely wounded were treated. This may hint at her burgeoning skills and the confidence that her superiors had in her abilities. Maud McCarthy comments on the heavy dressings undertaken in these wards and the need for these tasks to be performed by suitably trained professionals (as opposed to VADs). In pre-antibiotic days the often heavily contaminated wounds were irrigated with strong antiseptics (iodine, carbolic acid and mercury), with nurses always vigilant for the onset of gas gangrene which invariably led to amputation. Dressings could occur twice a day and nurses and patients alike often dreaded the agonising procedure.

That within a fortnight Beatrice was placed in charge of the 'lower half' of the ward – albeit where the slightly less seriously wounded were nursed – indicates that she was already showing the qualities her superiors would comment upon when she nursed at the Front: 'keen and interested in her work, reliable and conscientious.' She appears to have flourished under the early responsibility entrusted to her, whilst having the humility to seek advice when out of her depth.

Patients who finally recovered from their wounds would, in due course, be sent to a Command Depot before once again being returned to the Front. Although Beatrice does not record in her memoir having had such thoughts, many nurses, in the privacy of their letters, poems and diaries, questioned the part they were playing in simply patching men up so that they were fit enough to return to active service. Others record poignant farewells and anguish on hearing that a man they had coaxed back to life had been killed on returning to the Front.

Although most nurses found night duty, which often lasted for two to three months, arduous, Beatrice, in her usual cheerful manner, seems to have taken this in her stride, simply mentioning that she 'had had a very hard time' during night shifts. Responsibility for patients weighed heavily upon night staff. Beatrice had 'four huts of fifty beds each, assisted by one VAD in each'. It seems as though it was 'on nights' when recalcitrant male orderlies were most likely to fail to carry out orders. This may have presented Beatrice and others of her social background with difficulties, as initially she would have been more used to receiving than giving orders.

One orderly wrote in the hospital magazine, entitled *The Monthly Record of the 4th Northern General Hospital,* 'No petticoat government for me.' As the magazine's tone is frequently ironic, it is hard to know if this was intended as a tongue-in-cheek remark or not. However, I suspect not. Tensions between nurses and orderlies appeared to have run high in this, as in many hospitals, with both nurses and orderlies expressing veiled opinions about each other in the correspondence columns.

Various sources provide insight into what Beatrice would have contended with while working nights; the difficulties of adapting the body and the digestion to a nocturnal existence, or simply trying to get some rest when the majority of nurses were about their daily business. One nurse diarist, Sister Edith Appleton who served in France, comments that 'nurses are the most inconsiderate wretches under the sun, they tramp about, slam doors and pull plugs,' while night staff were endeavouring to rest.

Nurses on night duty also needed, at times, to decide whether to join in activities arranged on (rare) days off by colleagues and deprive themselves of sleep or forego the activities in order to rest. This seems to have been a particularly hard decision when overseas; Beatrice mentions at one point sharing an outing with friends and dropping off to sleep, just as a daytime raid seemed imminent.

In theory, when on home service nurses had three hours off-duty, from 9.30am to 12.30pm or 2.00pm to 5.00pm every day – work began on the wards at 7.00am and ended at 8.00pm. They were supposed to have a whole day off (from 6.00pm to 10.00pm the following day) every month and a weekly half-day (6.00pm to 10.00pm). When Beatrice is given her whole day plus half-day to spend with her 'Boy', her matron is being very kind.

Human beings are at their lowest ebb in the small hours of the morning and night staff frequently had more than their fair share of deaths to contend with. As night turned to day, night staff were expected to wake and wash patients, see that their beds were immaculately made, and hand-over to the day staff. Like other diarists, Beatrice comments on how convoys always seemed to arrive at night, placing further pressure on the already stretched skeleton night staff. If there was advance warning of convoys, then additional day staff could be drafted in but, with the vagaries of wartime transport, convoys could arrive hours later than expected, increasing sisters' administrative nightmares.

Although night duty could provide an opportunity for getting to know some of the patients, many memoirists write about the particular traumas of nursing those mentally as well as physically scarred by war, of how soldiers relived the horrors of their experiences as darkness enfolded them. More than one delusional patient had to be physically restrained from attempting to 'gas and kill the Boche'.

One poet nurse writes poignantly of the nightmares that crept up on patients when the lights were dimmed, leaving them dreading the night. For bereaved nurses, the quieter hours when patients slept were also hard to endure, as grief, which frenetically busy days kept slightly at bay, would creep up on them. Perhaps, as she sat in the dimness of the green-shaded night duty lamp, Beatrice mourned her brother Charles who had been killed in July 1916.

Religion: 'Help us to bear our Red Cross banner high'

Before 1914, within the British population of around 46 million, some 30 million citizens were nominally Anglican, while several million others followed the Roman Catholic and Non-conformist Christian doctrines. Church attendance was for countless families a weekly ritual; in many affluent homes the day often began and ended with the head of the household reading from the Bible. Children attended Sunday School on a weekly basis, prizes were awarded for high attendance and the words of the liturgy and of hymns were familiar to rich and poor alike. The Church's annual festivals punctuated the year and Biblical references and allusions were widely understood, offering comfort and reassurance in times of stress. Whilst turning some people away from religion, the war drew many people closer to their faith.

From the outset, the war was presented to the public as a Holy War: England and her Allies were engaged in a life and death struggle against the forces of evil, as manifested in Germany and the Central powers. Soldiers were often constructed in terms of modern day Crusaders, sometimes in terms of Christ Himself. Nurses, even in the often satirical magazine *Punch,* were depicted as serving in 'a holy shrine', whilst the prayer written for and given to every VAD by Rachel Crowdy, their

Commandant in France, linked (none too subtly) the volunteers' Red Cross with Christ's own, 'Lord, who once bore your own Cross shoulder high to save mankind, help us to bear our Red Cross banner high.'

Hospital days began with Prayers (at 6.30 am) and at 4NGH seem to have ended with a short Divine Service as well. Many nurses would have wanted to participate, regardless of whether this was compulsory. Certainly there is no sense that Beatrice felt compelled to attend but did so voluntarily, even when she had 'been frightfully busy all day'.

Army Chaplains (Padres) often record in their diaries the numbers of men coming forward for Confirmation. Padres often comforted the dying by telling them that if Christ could bear His agony on the Cross, so too could they bear theirs. Preserved postcards from across combatant nations depict Christ supporting wounded soldiers as they limp across the battlefields; those who were 'Hard Hit' were advised to 'Lean Hard'. During the war, many men recorded visions of Christ and their religious convictions sustained them during the war's darkest days. Women, especially mothers, irrespective of denomination, turned to Mary, the *Mater Dolorosa*, believing that she understood their personal torment. Hospital matrons were sometimes constructed, even by Anglicans, as 'the Madonna of our ward'.

For those serving in Roman Catholic France and Belgium, crucifixes and calvaries were ubiquitous; almost every village had at least one. Although many were destroyed when villages were shelled, others survived. Some serving personnel, both male and female, took comfort from these religious artefacts. For others, a near-destroyed statue of Christ was proof that even God had forsaken His people. When serving in France and Belgium, Beatrice would have seen many of these symbols, but the one that made the greatest impression upon her was the toppled statue of the Madonna and Child known as the Virgin of Albert.

The story of this statue, which has become an iconic image of the war, and to which Beatrice alludes after visiting Albert in 1918, is briefly told. Originally shelled and partially toppled by German artillery in January 1915, it was secured by the French at an angle of some 90 degrees. As Beatrice relates, the superstition developed on both sides that when the now horizontal statue finally fell, the war would shortly end with victory going to the side that had toppled her. When the bitterly fought-over Albert was briefly taken by the Germans in 1918, the British deliberately targeted and successfully toppled the Madonna, militarily, to prevent her being used as a look-out point but perhaps also to increase morale through the belief that the Allies would now win. She fell in August 1918.

Two contemporary poems about the Madonna are in stark contrast. One that Beatrice quotes by T.A. Girling is uplifting, whilst American volunteer on the Somme, Mary Borden's 'The Virgin of Albert' is one of the war's finest and most nihilistic poems. Borden describes the Virgin spiralling downwards towards the earth, clutching her child, with the terrible realisation that she has been betrayed, even by God.

It is against this background of religious conviction and Christian sacrifice (a soldier had died in her ward shortly beforehand and delayed her arrival at prayers) that what Beatrice calls her 'vision' of late May/early June 1916, when she imagines that she sees Christ standing beside a Cross, must be understood. This, and the profound effect it had upon her, may seem to today's readers weird or incomprehensible, but such an experience would not have struck her contemporaries or those she worked with as in any way strange. Soldiers, as well as civilians, frequently recounted their 'visions' in letters to and from the Front.

A few weeks after her vision, Beatrice learned of her beloved brother's death. Sapper 69983 Charles Hopkinson had volunteered in March 1915 and joined the Royal Engineers (RE), the regiment which in many ways formed the backbone of the British Army. His was almost certainly a hard war. A carpenter by trade, Charles' woodwork skills would have been much in demand, as it was the men of the RE who often tunnelled underground in an attempt to reach the German lines and detonate mines beneath the enemy trenches. They shored up the sides of these tunnels with wood.

On 2 July 1916 Charles was killed. He is buried in Maroeuil British Cemetery, along with 24 other officers and men of the RE tunnelling companies who died in mine explosions between March 1916 and the summer of 1918. Whether the information Beatrice received that his death was 'instantaneous' is accurate, is impossible to know; however, it is hard not to feel doubtful. Frequently, gruesome deaths at the Front were sanitised for those at home and Beatrice surely preferred to believe that her brother's end was quick. She, more than most who received the dreaded news, would have known the extent to which a mortally wounded man could suffer and how long it could take him to die even if, at this stage, she did not know that they might simply be left to die.

Beatrice gains strength from Charles' perceived visionary message with its Christian overtones, 'this I did for thee.' Like so many of the bereaved, her resolve was further strengthened by his sacrifice and she vowed to do all she could for those in her care. News of his death may have prompted her (as it did a number of women) to enrol as a TFNS nurse, as opposed to simply nursing soldiers at home; documents at the National Archives give her enlistment date as 19 July 1916.

Each time she attended prayers, Beatrice saw Charles' name inscribed on the small hospital chapel's Roll of Honour, funded by private subscription (with an additional loan) and opened in November 1915. A year later, according to the hospital magazine, the loan was still outstanding, although the Harvest Festival collection from both matins and evensong went some way towards paying it off. This recognition of Charles' sacrifice would have comforted Beatrice. Naming the dead is seen by some as a key component of the grief process. Even a century later, family members visiting a Commonwealth War Graves Commission headstone for the first time, almost invariably touch the chiselled name; it forms a tactile connection between the dead and the living.

Although little information remains about Charles' war service, RE Sapper Alexander Davidson's diaries have been preserved; he, like Charles, passed through the northern French village of Maroeuil. On 15 June 1916, when Alexander arrived there for the second time, he noted its transformation. Just weeks previously, there had at least been roofs over the dwellings where soldiers were billeted, now 'everything spoke of depression' and 'the cheerful attic window where I used to shave was hanging over the eaves.' Here, in this bleak spot, Charles Hopkinson spent the last weeks of his life and from here he responded to his sister's letter detailing her 'vision'.

The kindly matron who comforted Beatrice when she heard of Charles' death was TFNS Henrietta Ward, appointed Assistant Matron to 4NGH on 8 April 1915; three of her own seven serving brothers were killed between May and December 1915. She would have understood Beatrice's grief and undoubted concern for her remaining brother, Wilfred. It is tempting to assume that Beatrice already knew Henrietta, who in 1911 was a nurse at Nottingham General Hospital to which the fever wards were attached and where Beatrice would shortly enrol.

When announcing the happy news of Henrietta's June 1919 marriage to RAMC Lieutenant Colonel Lambert (a former administrator at 4NGH), *BJN* notes how 'very popular' she was, and the long list of wedding presents she received from her staff bears this out. In her married life, Henrietta took a keen interest in youth and other charitable organisations, such as the YMCA – perhaps she encouraged the 'Secret Society of Seven' which Beatrice writes about.

Running parallel with the ideals of Christian sacrifice that comforted Beatrice as she mourned Charles, were those of chivalry and heroism. Whilst these were instilled into public schoolboys through the curriculum, similar values were promoted amongst less privileged youngsters via organisations such as the YMCA (founded in 1844), YWCA, Boy Scouts, Girl Guides, Boys' and Girls' Brigades. The central tenet of these organisations was what has become known as 'muscular Christianity' – the belief that a healthy body creates a healthy mind and so the ideal way to achieve this moral and physical state is through outdoor activities and fellowship.

A sense of belonging to a group would have been important to soldier patients, with their deeply instilled loyalty to their regiment, company, and platoon. The 4NGH 'Secret Society of Seven' may have stimulated loyalty and fellowship, boosted patient morale and helped counter feelings of dislocation which hospitalised soldiers often felt. A long article in the 4th Northern General magazine of December 1916 describes members as having 'sipped the wine of good fellowship and felt the better for these sparkling times.' If given a choice, many soldiers preferred to go the same hospital as a 'mate', rather than be sent to one nearer their home, sometimes leaving relations to believe that the War Office was deliberately separating men from their families – a view still held today.

Serving Overseas: 'I was for Foreign Service'
In late spring 1917 Beatrice learned that she was 'for Foreign Service', a process she would have voluntarily initiated. On 25 April 1917, she had signed the 'Agreement for the Members of the TFNS who undertake to serve abroad if required during the present emergency.' She had pre-empted by two days Lord Derby's appeal to nurses to volunteer for service with the military and his reference to the 'Nursing Service's glorious record ... to which the country owes such a debt of gratitude.'

Despite the urgency of the appeal, it would take several weeks before the 19 4NGH members were finally on their way. The three sisters and six staff nurses included South African national Mary Ochse, who was in

England when war broke out and offered her services to the war effort, and 10 VADs. They took with them the good wishes of those involved with the hospital magazine and the hope that 'they may have the strength to carry on their work.' In London they met the additional 72 nurses drawn from amongst the best of the other four Northern Command Military Hospitals, including 2NGH.

The nurses would have been wearing TFNS uniform dresses of blue-grey 'washing' material (sturdy, colour-fast cotton), with a white linen collar and cuffs and white muslin cap. A silver service badge with the 'double-A' cypher of Queen Alexandra would be clearly visible on the right lapel of their 'blue-grey cape with scarlet facings', and a silver 'T' (costing 2s 9d) at each corner. At least one 4NGH Tommy quipped that these stood for 'Tommies' Tormentors!' The nurses themselves preferred the acronym 'Thoroughly Trained'.

After the war, TFNS nurses were not automatically allowed to keep their 'T' badges. Correspondence directed towards Beatrice in 1920 requests the return of hers, as she had completed only three of the required four years' service. A further document confirms that she complied. One must assume she did so with a heavy heart. Subsequently the rule was relaxed, and in December 1923, Beatrice received a letter telling her that those who had completed two years' service could retain their badge 'as a memento of war service'. The word 'memento', doubtless unintentionally, seems to trivialise the experience, dedication and utter professionalism of these formerly civilian nurses.

A velour hat formed part of the TFNS outdoor uniform. These rather natty headpieces caused some conflict, as neither QAIMNS nor VADs were sanctioned to wear them. Nor, despite some nurses hoping they might be, were fur collars allowed; McCarthy suggested that 'a suitable uniform Macintosh would be a great boon.' Nurses were given £8 5s to cover the cost of their uniform and an additional £7 10s for camp equipment, which included a portable camp bedstead and '1 Tripod washstand with proofed basin, bag and bath.' There would be countless times when Beatrice was unable to avail herself of these.

Nurses were expected to provide their own instruments and the size of their trunk was stipulated. Non-essential items were paid for out of their own pockets. When TFNS nurses were told to report to their designated hospitals for the first time, they were reminded, 'Uniform only is to be taken; no plain clothes are required.' The lack of need for civilian clothes may explain why, three years later, when returning to Civvy Street Beatrice 'had no civilian clothes at all'.

If Beatrice and her colleagues had followed veteran Violetta Thurstan's advice, then their luggage would have included additional practical items. Violetta advised warm pyjamas, 'much more useful garments than the be-ribboned nightgowns made of thin cambric which are sometimes brought.' Furthermore:

> [a] *sun umbrella is a great comfort in hot weather. Plenty of stockings are necessary; very thin ones are a mistake, they are cold in winter, mosquitoes bite through them in summer, and they always want mending. Galoshes are dull but very necessary. Gum boots lined with felt are indispensable for camping. A woollen jersey, of the same colour as the uniform is generally allowed, and serves also as a bed-jacket in cold weather.*

Despite Violetta's stricture to travel light, her long list of potentially useful items included 'carbolised Vaseline for blisters', as through her own lengthy overseas service she knew that nurses were run off their feet. She also recommended a 'Tommy's cooker' (a very small portable stove powered, often ineffectively, by solidified alcohol). These were widely advertised in the press as, 'A suitable gift to the men in the trenches'. The ever-resourceful Beatrice mentions having one but, as old soldiers could have told her, boiling the water took a long time. It is unsurprising that her own cup of tea made on the train to Folkestone was 'welcome' when she finally got it.

Beatrice seems to have been lucky, as throughout her headlong rush to multiple CCS, her luggage always seemed to turn up. Many nurses lost theirs and McCarthy's diaries make frequent mention of attempts to find or recompense nurses for luggage gone astray.

Although the 92 women were fearful of both occurrences, they were neither 'torpedoed nor sea-sick' on the crossing. The latter would have been an inconvenience, the former a genuine threat. By 1917, significant numbers of ships had been lost to German U-boat activity. That their ship, *Victoria*, was convoyed indicates that this risk was present in the minds of the authorities. Although little archival information appears to exist about *Victoria*, she was not a hospital ship, as she was carrying servicemen (hospital ships could not carry troops returning to combat duties, only the wounded on their way home, yet medical personnel could be carried in both directions) making her especially vulnerable. Beatrice was understandably excited; the atmosphere amongst troops returning from leave would have been less ebullient.

On arrival in Boulogne, nurses were met not by a sergeant-major barking orders at them, but by Matron Isabel Woodford TFNS, the Embarkation Sister. Her duties included: ensuring that nurses' luggage was dealt with; accommodation was provided for them; 'all irregularities in uniform' checked; and that nurses were helped 'in every way possible'. Isabel would have also assisted those departing on leave, so Beatrice may have had contact with her on several occasions.

With hundreds of nurses of all nationalities flocking into and departing from Boulogne, the Embarkation Sister's duties were considerable; she covered miles on a daily basis, criss-crossing Boulogne's cobbled streets. The logistical work required to get nurses to their designated hospitals, Casualty Clearing Stations, Ambulance Trains and barges is often overlooked, yet the smooth-running of this 'back office' was integral to the nursing effort. There was nothing *ad hoc* about the nursing services in France, largely thanks to Maud McCarthy's superb administrative skills. Sadly, the records of the nurses who passed through Boulogne before August 1918 were destroyed when Base HQ was bombed on 1 August 1918.

Isabel sent Beatrice and her party to Hotel 'Louve' (sic: Louvre); Beatrice was unimpressed by its stuffy, overcrowded atmosphere – British nurses were renowned for believing in the healing properties of fresh air and decent lavatories, 'foreigners' less so. Used consistently by the army and the Medical Services since August 1914, McCarthy always found this establishment's directors 'most accommodating'. Countless diaries refer to personnel spending the night there. In order to facilitate the dispatch of nurses to their onward destinations, the Louvre made a dining-room available for them to be processed as quickly as possible.

Exploring Boulogne, Beatrice was disconcerted by the foreignness. Although the food tasted different, she was delighted to find there appeared to be few shortages. There was even 'butter', not margarine, which was now a hated staple of English wartime diets. By 1917, food shortages in England were a real concern; starvation was on the horizon. Tons of imported foodstuffs were lost at sea to enemy attacks and Food Riots had broken out in several cities. The King exhorted his subjects to 'Eat Less Food', and recipe leaflets suggesting delicacies such as 'nettle purée' were available. Beatrice and her colleagues were thrilled to be able to buy 'cakes with rich icings' in France. Sugar, the first food to be rationed in England, had been restricted to 12 oz a week, and only one fresh egg a week, if available, was allowed, though this was more likely to be fortnightly. Beatrice thoughtfully took some French food when travelling home on leave in early 1918.

During the war, Britain sent some 3,240,948 tons of food to the Western Front. Some of it was unappreciated – although the army diet was better than poorer soldiers were used to, and certainly better than the fare being eaten by many people at home by 1918. Amongst the most lampooned army dishes were the infamous plum and apple jam, 'beef' and vegetable stew (maconochie), which often consisted of low grade meat with globules of lard floating on the top, and the 'bully beef' which Beatrice mentions. Although in the earlier days, troops up the line had been supplied by ration parties, this had become hazardous. 'Death by Dixie' was all too common, as ration parties were shelled and killed, so troops in the trenches became dependent on basic army rations which could be heated on the spot. By late 1918, Beatrice sometimes lived on these due to difficulties with provisioning CCS. Perhaps she still had her 'Tommy's cooker' to heat her rations up.

Mabel Leigh Whiffin: 'a matron of exceptional ability'

Although Beatrice never gives her matrons' names, her first overseas matron was Mabel Leigh Whiffin, of 2 Northern General Hospital (Leeds) (2NGH), which along with Lincoln, Leicester, Sheffield and Newcastle formed the hospitals of the army's 'Northern Command'. From Beatrice's own spontaneous comments and Mabel's service file at the National Archives, a fascinating picture emerges of a woman who surely ranked amongst the TFNS' finest nurses. As her confidential records note, she not only had a talent for 'organizing and administering' but also an 'intimate knowledge … of the capabilities of her nursing staff,' which allowed her to recognise potential – as she did in Beatrice's case – and bring out the best in her staff.

Born in 1868 in Dovercourt, Essex, Mabel was the daughter of the Paymaster-in-Chief to the Royal Navy. Despite serving with the TFNS, Mabel would have been, in terms of social standing and training, the perfect QAIMNS recruit. Within nine years of training at St Thomas', one of the London Teaching Hospitals, she had achieved the rank of matron.

Her referees praised both her administrative and organisational qualities as well as her being 'extremely nice to work with'.

2NGH was a large hospital with 1,900 beds, overseen by 222 trained and 165 untrained staff. Mabel may have viewed it as a stepping-stone to an overseas appointment. A 1915 referee wrote, 'all her people have been in the army or the navy and so she is keen to do what she can for the War.' It is to Mabel's credit that she made so favourable an impression on staff and patients when she joined the hospital in Leeds in 1915. Correspondence between TFNS Matron-in-Chief, Sydney Browne, and Principal Matron Euphemia Innes prior to Mabel's arrival indicates that Innes and the RAMC officers were apparently 'extremely sorry' that a different lady had not been appointed.

When Mabel went overseas, Euphemia Innes wrote of being 'very sorry to lose her' but, like many matrons, acknowledged that 'we must give of our best to France'. It is likely that Beatrice's hospital also felt they were giving of their best when she departed in September 1917; she too would prove her worth. Far more nurses applied for foreign service than were accepted; those who, like Beatrice and Mabel, were taken on and remained overseas often showed particular abilities.

Beatrice's first insight into Mabel's character occurs in the memoir at a point when she hardly knew her. Her broad-mindedness, also commented on by Mabel's RAMC Commanding Officer (CO), Colonel F. H. Westmacott, endeared her to the excited young nurses, most of whom were about to have their first taste of foreign travel, let alone active service overseas. How thankful they were to find that 'our Matron speaks French.' On the outward journey, Beatrice noted, 'Matron had been so kind to us.'

When the kindly Mabel took her nurses to France in 1917, the war had been dragging on for three years; conditions, and morale, were at a low point and nursing personnel were faced with situations unimaginable pre-1914. Mabel remained a kind and steadying influence. During the air raids where Beatrice herself would prove steadfast, Mabel always came round to chat with patients and staff and keep their spirits up. Patients and nurses admired her ability to be a calming presence when all hell was let loose overhead, yet this restraint subsequently took its toll on Mabel.

Mabel seems to have understood the need to maintain morale. During a sports day held by one of the nearby Units (these were regular entertainments, generally put on by soldiers 'at rest' behind the lines for their own and, if possible, nurses' amusement), Beatrice competed in and won a 'flat race' and came second in the sack race. Although most matrons allowed their nurses to watch, many forbade competing; Mabel, however, understanding the psychological importance of recreation in times of stress, encouraged her staff to participate.

Again unlike some matrons, she welcomed 'the boys' who attended the 'At Homes' she allowed her nurses to organise. These were the only events where nurses and servicemen could meet socially. In the restricted atmosphere of the Army Nursing Service, any contact between the sexes was controlled and chaperoned. 'At Homes' with a tolerant matron provided both genders with precious moments of near-normality.

There was one rule Mabel was powerless to change. Dancing, for British Army nurses, was forbidden throughout the war, at least partly out of fear of possible sexual scandals which had been foretold by those who were against women being, in the words of Elizabeth Haldane (sister of Lord Haldane, the Secretary of State for War and a member of the TFNS original council), 'thrown into the turmoil and excitement of war.'

Although some nurses did circumvent the interdiction, those who were caught dancing were hauled in front of Maud McCarthy, Matron-in-Chief to the BEF, and generally transferred to another hospital or even back to England, where their conduct was closely monitored. Despite the Deputy Director of Medical Services (DDMS) being, 'strongly in favour' of a little dancing, McCarthy over-ruled him. In her opinion, 'while we were engaged in the work we were doing at the present time, I considered dancing was out of place ... Either the sick and wounded were going to be nursed, or we were going to dance' (4 October 1917). In their heart of hearts, Beatrice and Mabel assuredly felt that nurses could manage to do both.

This interdiction rumbled on; it was discussed by the matrons-in-chief of the Dominion and US Nursing Services. The Canadian matron-in-chief placed on record that, 'she considered dancing a necessary and very legitimate exercise and that Nurses who were surrounded with an atmosphere of depression needed the recreation both mentally and physically,' (23 November 1917). Unsurprisingly, McCarthy's voice held sway amongst British nurses; dancing remained prohibited until a temporary relaxation of the rules 'for this exceptional Christmas [*1918*]'. This concession was, according to McCarthy, 'greatly appreciated'.

This levity was not to be repeated, for, on 31 January 1919, McCarthy stated categorically: 'I said it [*dancing*] could not be. Either we were going to look after the patients or the nurses were going to enjoy themselves, and in addition it was a very bad example to civil nurses who had been attached to the Reserve or TFNS and who would shortly be returning to their civil employment where such things as constant dances were not considered suitable.' Beatrice's granddaughter remembers being told about all the rules and regulations with which Beatrice had to comply during her training. Dancing, or its interdiction, was undoubtedly amongst them.

Despite Mabel being 'Mentioned in Dispatches', an honour of which she was 'very proud', her overseas service ended before Beatrice's. Following leave in England in December 1918, she was once again instructed to report for permanent duty at 2NGH in January 1919. She had set those under her command a superb example of wartime leadership coupled with humanity. Telegrams had flown between GHQ France and the Director of Medical Services in England during her leave. Despite hoping to return to France, she was 'urgently required for an important appointment.' It may have been that she was a victim of her own success. She had been removed from 59GH and sent to run 57GH in Marseilles, as this hospital, according to McCarthy, was not 'running satisfactorily, certain irregularities having occurred.'

It is unclear precisely what happened but, on 19 December 1920, Principal Matron Innes wrote, in evident distress, to Dame Maud McCarthy, informing her that 'poor Miss Whiffin', who had been on duty until 11 December, had 'had a complete mental breakdown.' Innes' anguish is apparent, she begs the illustrious McCarthy to 'do something', as it is 'heart breaking to see her now.' She states explicitly that this breakdown, which would now be termed post-traumatic stress disorder, was caused by Miss Whiffin's war service, recounting in some detail how, 'in her wanderings [*Mabel*] imagines and talks of air raids.' Innes adds that the 'doctors in charge of her case' were also adamant that her illness was caused by her war service.

Innes, who does not appear to have served overseas, seems a little surprised (although deeply sympathetic) that one who always appeared 'calm and collected and full of care for others' could be so traumatised. The countless nurses who shared Mabel's and Beatrice's experiences may have been less surprised. Innes concludes 'it is all so terribly sad and we are all very upset. Every man or woman who worked with [*her*] admired her greatly.' Mabel's was not an isolated case; recent doctoral research has revealed the very significant numbers of nursing personnel diagnosed with neurasthenia (shell-shock) either during or after the war.

Despite initial hopes that this measure would not be necessary, Mabel was transferred to a mental hospital for specialist care. Perhaps testimony both to the treatment and to her own resilient character, and despite an initially gloomy prognosis, she recovered sufficiently to work again. She did not resume her role as Matron of the busy Leeds Hospital, but on 24 August 1921 she writes to 'Dear Dame Maud', who had continued to be interested in her progress, that she was now in charge of 'two houses which are occupied by the nursing staff of the Ministry of Pensions Hospital'.

Post-war these establishments were not military hospitals (although many had been during the war), and instead they had been opened for the care of severely wounded ex-service personnel. Whether this was an ideal environment for one whose nerves were now fragile is doubtful. Mabel hopes that 'when she is quite settled [*she*] will be very happy here,' but currently she tells McCarthy, 'everything is quite strange but all are most kind to me.'

At this juncture Mabel's nursing record fades from history, apart from her gaining a seat on the recently founded General Nursing Council for England and Wales. However, the concern, even love, and admiration her peers felt for Mabel surfaced following her sudden death on 3 November 1928. The Queen (who sent a personal letter), the Director General of Army Medical Services, and Dame Ann Beardsmore-Smith, now TFNS Matron-in-Chief, as well as the wider nursing community condoled with Mabel's sister, Alice.

Did Beatrice, by then in distant Washington, learn of the death of the matron whom she had revered and who, in turn, had considered the young staff nurse to be 'steady, reliable, cheerful'? Both Mabel and Beatrice had these qualities in abundance.

Nursing in France at 'A place called St Omer'

When Beatrice and her colleagues discovered they were going to St Omer they may have been unaware that this town, some 45 miles from Boulogne, had been the BEF headquarters between August 1914 and March 1916. Its position on the lines of communication (the vital route that connects an operating military unit with its supply base and along which supplies and reinforcements are carried), made it vulnerable to attack and even to espionage.

In wartime, information about what is occurring along lines of communication provides the enemy with vital intelligence. The authorities were constantly on the alert for spies; apocryphal 'spy' stories abounded, including signalling apparently carried out by placing different garments on washing lines and, early on in the war, fears that posters advertising German products could conceal hidden messages. When Beatrice arrived these would have long disappeared.

By 1917, St Omer had become a main hospital base for British and Colonial Stationary and General Hospitals. Although there appears to be no record as to when the hospital to be numbered 59GH was proposed, the first reference to its imminent opening occurs in McCarthy's 8 July 1917 diary entry: 'accommodation was now ready for the nursing staff – informed DGMS by wire, and asked that the entire staff might be sent out and notification of embarkation might be wired direct to this office.' This 'now' might reveal why Beatrice's orders for overseas service had taken so long to come through and appeared so contradictory. Her designated hospital was, quite simply, not operational.

Once staff arrived on 14 July, it was important to ensure that the hospital was rapidly made operational. The Third Battle of Ypres was imminent and the high casualty projections proved tragically accurate. Widely known as Passchendaele and launched on 31 July 1917, it aimed to destroy German submarine bases on the north coast of Belgium; submarines were responsible for the sinking of countless ships and the loss of hundreds of tons of imported foodstuffs. McCarthy's deputy (McCarthy herself was recovering from appendectomy) visited 59GH on 15 July. She:

saw Miss Whiffin, the Matron and the nursing staff who had arrived the night before. Went over the hospital with the Matron and the CO. The hospital is a large building to accommodate 1,000 patients, recently used as a hospital by the French. There are beds for 40 officers in the building and there is also an Officers' Hospital about 4 miles out, with 100 beds. The Sisters are all temporarily accommodated in a large school intended later to be used as part of the hospital, for minor cases.

In this 'large school' Beatrice and the five Lincoln staff nurses excitedly chose their room and began adjusting to being on active service.

Coming from a large family, Beatrice may not have found sharing a room with five other women problematic. Many affluent VADs found the lack of privacy a particularly trying aspect of war service, although others, nurses and VADs, found sharing helped bolster their morale or even that it forced a mask of bravery during air raids.

On 20 August 1917 Beatrice was working in the thick of war, for the Germans bombed Hazebrouck, a crucial British-held rail centre about 14 miles east of St Omer. 'Between 7 p.m. and midnight 1,000 to 1,200 patients were sent down the line. The sisters left the next morning for St. Omer,' (McCarthy). Whilst the condition of the patients pouring in would have alerted Beatrice to the full reality of front line nursing, the now homeless New Zealand nurses billeted on 59GH would also have informed their colleagues about working up the line as battle raged nearby.

St Omer itself was soon under attack; this would last for a month. On 2 September, an Australian nurse (May Tilton), working in a St Omer CCS noted how 'nine enemy [*aircraft*] took part in the raid which was favoured by the bright moonlight.' Two days later, she notes bombs dropping in the hospital 'enclosure reserved for Officers and Nursing Sisters … three large bombs dropped in a field not far off.' Raids continued throughout September, 'as long as the moon lasted, the air raids lasted.'

Nurses, including Beatrice, came to hate the moonlight. It is ironic that the moon was then so bright, as the summer of 1917 was the wettest and coldest on record in northern France and Belgium, and the military action around Ypres was fought in a quagmire of mud. Nurses up the line had to contend with the discomforts of the weather, as well as the dangers of bombs and shellfire. They, like the troops, were surrounded by mud and many suffered from chilblains and trench foot. One doctor remarked that some sisters' feet were as 'bad if not worse than their patients'.

Fortunately, as it would turn out, in late September the 59GH nurses were moved out of their school building to permanent accommodation in General Pétain's house, which he had vacated. McCarthy was unimpressed by the living conditions, '68 nurses were crammed into the available accommodation,' and 'the rooms were so full that it was impossible to get in all the trunks' (each one 30 x 24 x 12 inches). To enable all the staff to be accommodated in one unit, 'huts are being put up in the grounds to accommodate 20 nurses.' One must hope that the nurses had brought the warm pyjamas Violetta Thurstan had recommended.

To McCarthy's fury, the quartermaster was being miserly over allocating coal, light and 'more than one blanket, and this he only gave as a favour.' The cheerful Beatrice glosses over these inconveniences in her memoir. McCarthy was critical of Matron Whiffin, who McCarthy felt was rather slumming it with her staff, as opposed to living in a proffered separate house – apparently, Mabel 'preferred to have all her staff together.' Small wonder that she endeared herself to her nurses. 'We all loved her,' Beatrice wrote subsequently – an unusual accolade for a matron.

Air raids became a recurrent part of Beatrice's war experience. With Passchendaele raging, with troops constantly moving through to the battlefront, and with the presence of heavy workshops and tank laagers in the city, as well as a high number of Air Service personnel and flying squadrons, St Omer was a key target. The 59GH sergeant's initial orders to personnel about extinguishing lights had been deadly serious. 'Night air raids were frequent, and patients, orderlies and nursing staff had some narrow escapes from injury in the canvas section of the hospital. Sisters and orderlies wore tin hats while on duty,' noted McCarthy.

Beatrice would come to appreciate the psychological as well as physical protection these helmets offered; she mentions being given one, along with a gas mask. By 1917 these too were routinely issued to nurses – some nurses gave their masks to soldiers returning to front line duties, occasionally with severe consequences for themselves. At least one American nurse, Helen Fairchild, is known to have died as a direct result of gas poisoning and it almost certainly contributed to the deaths of a number of others. Nurses often suffered the after-effects of proximity to a soldier who had been gassed, as his uniform would be permeated with the deadly fumes which nurses would inhale when they undressed him.

Beatrice describes the air raid which occurred on 30 September in chilling and extensive detail. 59GH got off more lightly than the nearby tented 58GH, which took a direct hit. Following attacks earlier in the month, attempts had been made to open up nearby caves and create shelters for this hospital's staff and ambulant patients, yet the casualty toll was considerable. Twenty-two patients and four nurses were killed: Staff Nurse Agnes Climie (TFNS), Sister Mabel Milne (TFNS), and VADs Daisy Coles and Elizabeth Thomson. They, like so many medical casualties from St Omer, lie in nearby Longuenesse Cemetery.

Following the 30 September attack, 58GH staff were billeted to two other hospitals, including 59GH, now bursting at the seams. Although on this terrible night 59GH suffered less than 58GH, the annexe where Beatrice and her colleagues had originally been accommodated, 'was absolutely destroyed.' Fortunately, these patients were all walking cases and had already been evacuated to the cellars. However, as Beatrice reported, the telephone orderly on duty was killed and the building itself entirely wrecked, with doors off their hinges, cupboards smashed, windows broken and most of the beds smashed to the ground.

Hospitals of all sorts, should, as neutral facilities with the Red Cross clearly displayed, have been exempt from attack but the international symbol of charity and neutrality provided little protection. Regarding the bombing of hospitals, the German High Command retorted that if these were sited close to railway lines (legitimate targets), then the Allies had only themselves to thank if one were struck.

Beatrice and other diarists mention the prisoner-of-war camp in St Omer, where a significant number of the 7,000 prisoners captured since June 1917 were accommodated. Wounded POWs were treated in Allied hospitals where some nurses, initially at least, resented having to care for them. The arrival of 500 wounded Germans at 58GH was seen as particularly problematic, due to the recent bombing and loss of life. Although not prioritised for operations (at one point Beatrice mentions that they knew they were nearing the end of their interminable duties in the operating theatre because the German prisoner-patients were being brought in), prisoners received identical nursing care to Allied wounded, whilst being nursed in separate wards. However, their beds were placed far apart to prevent them from speaking to each other.

Generally, as time passed and they became more involved with an individual's care, nurses who had initially been reluctant to nurse them began to see prisoners as wounded men first and Germans second. One QAIMNS(R) nurse was severely reprimanded for handing an envelope to a German patient who, on release, wished to keep in touch with her. Her CO intercepted his subsequent letter thanking her for her kindness. Strictly against regulations (GRO 1839) this was constructed as fraternising with the enemy.

Despite the stresses of their work, which by early October – with the continuous air raids as well as the usual demands of nursing – was taking physical and mental toll, nurses found ways of getting around the local area on their (about fortnightly) half-days off. 'Lorry-hopping', whilst strictly forbidden, was the ideal method both of sight-seeing and forgetting for a few glorious hours the horrors of the wards and the fears of the nightly attacks. Like many of her colleagues, Beatrice loved this activity. One must assume that Mabel turned a blind eye to the practice. It is unsurprising that some women later found the post-war world horribly tame; a part of them yearned for the excitement and freedom of their wartime lives, referred to by one serving female poet as 'dear dead days that will not come again.'

Clubs providing simple but welcome home comforts also allowed some respite from the hospitals and their suffering. Beatrice joined the St Omer branch of the Princess Victoria's Rest Clubs for Nurses, which had been established at 22 Rue de Wissococq in July 1917. 'This Club was specially appreciated by the large number of travelling Sisters who were passing through St Omer on their way to front areas and who often remained there several days in reserve until they received orders,' according to McCarthy. As well as these transient nurses moving up and down the lines on Ambulance Trains, Hospital Barges, and to and from CCS, by October 1917, 300 nurses were permanently established in St Omer. When the ADMS ordered its closure in April, 1918, 'on account of the continuous air-raids, and the military situation in general,' this would have been a real loss for all St Omer nurses and doctors.

Other organisations also provided a semblance of home for servicemen and women. Probably the most famous of these was the YMCA, which Beatrice always appreciated, often finding their huts in unlikely places. Staffed by women as well as men, the YMCA established very temporary havens in ruined houses, barns, cellars and dug-outs, distributing hot drinks, Bovril and Oxo, biscuits, cakes, cigarettes, and notepaper. There are still countless letters in private and public collections written on paper with the distinctive red triangle and YMCA logo in the centre. Perhaps Beatrice herself penned a few lines home, confident that the staff would send it on its way. In September 1917, King George told Sir Arthur Yapp, the YMCA's National Secretary, 'You have placed the whole Empire under a debt to you.' Thousands of personnel would have agreed.

At one YMCA hut Beatrice and her colleagues signed the officer-in-charge's autograph book. Very significant numbers of war workers kept autograph books and a few have been preserved. Some signatories just wrote their name, others composed poems, wrote notes, drew pictures and recorded their thoughts, hopes, gratitude and longings. Books that survive are poignant reminders of lives lived under the shadow of death. Maybe somewhere in a private or museum collection one bears the autograph, 'Beatrice Harriet Hopkinson.'

If lorry-hopping, the YMCA and also the St Omer Nurses' Club, which Beatrice had naturally joined, provided brief moments of entertainment, her nursing duties were still always Beatrice's priority. At 59GH, after completing night duty, she gained experience in the operating theatre which would stand her in excellent stead when she moved to various CCS. General Hospital operating work was demanding. Teams of surgeons worked round the clock, sometimes for days on end, striving to save the lives, if not the limbs, of those on the (often five or six) tables in front of them.

Surgeons' records mention the sheer physical and, indeed, mental exhaustion of their work, the burden of which was increased, according to one Base Hospital surgeon, by endless forms, regulations and red tape. Nurses who anticipated surgeons' needs, as Beatrice learned to do, would have been greatly appreciated. At times, the surgical teams were so pressed that dentists, nurses, even Padres, were pressed into service as anaesthetists.

The praise Beatrice earned for her work in CCS operating theatres would have made a less modest person proud. M. C. Corbishley RRC, OBE, the sister-in-charge of 58CCS, wrote that Beatrice was 'keen and interested in her work, reliable, conscientious, energetic and punctual.' Lieutenant-Colonel Graham Martin (RAMC) concurred, adding, 'she has done excellent work in the Operating Theatre. She is very quick … and takes the greatest trouble to anticipate the surgeon's needs.' Not only was she efficient, she was, crucially, 'kind and considerate to the patients.'

By the time these comments were written Beatrice had discovered that operations performed in CCS took surgeons' and nurses' skills into a whole new realm, for she and her team arrived at their first CCS as the war entered its most critical and, for the Allies, most precarious stage. With the military situation changing by the day, even by the hour, Beatrice was too busy to know what was going on. She could, however, see with her own eyes a 'constant stream of traffic; lorries; ambulances; cars; guns; soldiers in column marching to and from the front line; civilians on the retreat; and wounded soldiers limping down from the field ambulance … [*all endeavouring*] to get away from the "Hades".' Operations Michael and Georgette were being unleashed and Beatrice and her CCS colleagues were soon caught up in them.

'Fleeing before their onslaught': Operations Michael & Georgette, March – April 1918

By the beginning of 1918, after almost four years of war, France, Germany, Great Britain and Russia were economically on their knees and the very fabric of European society was showing alarming signs of collapse. Russia had suffered a revolution that effectively removed her from the war; France's armies had mutinied, following the disastrous Nivelle offensive in 1917; Great Britain was seriously concerned that she might be starved into submission, thanks to the German submarine campaign threatening her vital supply lines (and which the Battle of Passchaendaele had failed to resolve); Germany was plagued with socialist unrest, poor morale and rebellion at home.

Russia's withdrawal allowed Germany to transfer her armies from the East to the Western Front and by superior numbers of three to one, threaten to potentially overwhelm France and Great Britain. The German military commanders knew that they had to act promptly before the Americans – who had entered the war in April 1917 but were not yet in France – were able to bring their might to the conflict, which would spell certain defeat for Germany.

Germany's daring plan was to attack the Allies on two fronts, split the French from the British and seize the railheads in Amiens in the south and Hazebrouck in the north. In March 1918, Operation Michael opened on the Somme front with astounding results. Specially trained Storm Troops smashed through the overstretched defensive lines of the British to a depth of up to 40 miles – a huge success when victory had previously been counted in hundreds of yards. Only by resolve were the British able to contain the chaos and hold the German attack, before it ran out of steam and outran supply lines, bringing German troops to a standstill.

In the north, Operation Georgette was unleashed in April 1918 and again achieved quite amazing results, causing panic within the Allied command. Armentières fell, as did Béthune, before Field Marshal Sir Douglas Haig, Commander in Chief of the British Army, issued his 'Backs to the Wall' order, telling his soldiers to fight to the last man in an attempt to halt the German offensive which, at that point, appeared unstoppable.

The appointment of French Marshal Ferdinand Foch as Allied Supreme Commander finally unified the Allies' defence, as Germany struggled against huge losses and to maintain her gains against an enemy that was growing more powerful month by month, as American involvement started to bite.

A third German offensive in May 1918, intended as a diversion to draw off British reserves from the north, was unleashed against the British and French south of the Aisne River on the Chemin des Dames. It was within 37 miles of Paris before being halted by the first deployment of half-trained American forces and a determined French defence, which eventually repelled the attackers.

Through total exhaustion and not least the ability of the Allies to initially absorb the massive German attacks on two fronts, Germany failed in her attempt to end the conflict in her favour. Overwhelming Allied counter offensives in July and August 1918 resulted in the 'Hundred Days' that eventually brought about the collapse of the German war machine and forced the German Army, battered but defiant, back within its borders. An agreed ceasefire, rather than a total surrender, was signed on 11 November 1918 bringing the Great War to an arranged conclusion, although not a definite defeat for the German military. This attempt to save further bloodshed led, through the punitive terms of the Treaty of Versailles, to a further war 20 years later.

Nursing Near the Front: Casualty Clearing Stations

Before serving at her first CCS and being swept up in the full force of the early days of this German advance, Beatrice went home on her delayed two weeks' leave (leave was supposed to occur every six months). Many nurses eagerly awaited leave and its postponement, not infrequent if there were a 'big push', was dreaded. However, once back home many service personnel found a chasm now existed between those who had been 'at the Front' and folk at home. Almost perversely, they then longed to return to their theatre of war, to be with those who understood their experiences. This appears not to have been the case for Beatrice, who enjoyed her holiday.

To Beatrice's delight, her orders came through: she was to be posted to 62CCS in Proven or Bandaghem (known to the troops as 'Bandage 'Em'), Belgium. Many nurses yearned for service in a CCS, but selection criteria were strict, based on confidential reports, previous service and record of health. In the many CCS where she served Beatrice would intimately experience the full horrors of this most brutal war.

By the time Beatrice reported for her (brief) duty at 62CCS in early spring 1918, these had evolved into large, complex but very competent medical facilities, where the wounded were 'processed' as quickly and efficiently as humanly possible. Grouped together in twos and threes with accommodation for between 800 to 1,200 wounded, the practice was to fill one CCS up, before rotating to the next. According to Dr Tom Scotland, during Passchendaele (July-November 1917), there were '24 CCS with 379 doctors, 502 nursing sisters.' They 'processed over 200,000 casualties and operated on 61,423 of them.'

In *Everyman At War* (1930), Surgeon John Hayward provides a graphic account of a CCS operating theatre where some surgeons could get through 15 to 20 operations in a 12-hour shift. Nurses who, like Beatrice, could anticipate a surgeon's requirements, were greatly appreciated. CCS operating theatres were broadly similar: twin operating tables, each team working 16 hours on, 8 hours off, at which point, as Beatrice makes clear, the exhausted staff crawled to whatever shelter they could find, to try to snatch some rest.

John Hayward found it, 'impossible to convey an adequate picture of the scene. Into the tent are borne on stretchers, or come wearily stumbling, figures in khaki, wrapped in blankets or coats, bandaged or splinted. All of them stiff with mud, or caked with blood and dust, and salt sweat, and with labels of their injuries attached.' Medical staff strove to create some order, whilst making decisions to prioritise those who might perhaps have a chance of life over those for whom no hope remained. Few could previously have 'seen such frightful wounds.' They would have little time to deal with them.

Beatrice was forewarned that she was for 'teamwork' and introduced to the medical officer with whom she would work. Each team consisted of surgeon, anaesthetist, sister, and trained orderly; they were sent as rapid reinforcements in response to SOS calls from other CCS. A contemporary document in the Australian War Memorial describes how members were 'trained to work together.' They would be called for by a CCS which found itself overwhelmed by urgent cases and then return to their 'home' CCS to await the next rush of patients elsewhere.

Certainly Beatrice's teamwork coincided with a time of 'great stress'. Perhaps she had been selected for duty in vulnerable spots, as Mabel

Whiffin had noted in her confidential report that she was 'very level-headed during air-raids.' The last thing a CCS needed was a nurse who panicked. As Beatrice had noticed, patients often took their cue from nurses during attacks. If nurses managed to remain outwardly calm, so did they. Beatrice's abilities were about to be put to the test.

Five days after arriving at 62CCS, a call came through from 47CCS, Rosières which had, in August 1917, experienced being in the thick of battle. Five sisters had subsequently been sent down the line suffering from shell-shock. Rosières was once again vulnerable as, by 24 March, the German advance was closing in; 47CCS had already received orders to be ready to pack up and retreat at a moment's notice, whilst still fulfilling its obligations to the wounded. Now they needed to retreat – and fast. Allied medical facilities, as well as Allied soldiers, were truly on the run.

Beatrice and her colleagues fell back to Amiens (with its vital railway links), which was still in Allied hands, but the battle followed them. Her descriptions are graphic, as the military situation deteriorated and the German advance seemed unstoppable. Evacuating CCS were pouring into Amiens, and many, like Beatrice, were sent to 42 Stationary Hospital, around which there was 'continual bombing' according to Matron-in-Chief McCarthy. On 26 March, 42 Stationary was ordered to evacuate. Beatrice and her team were not alone in wondering if defeat was now in sight.

Eventually Beatrice's team were posted back to their original, albeit re-located, CCS, 62CCS. Although Beatrice does not mention this aspect of the situation, McCarthy's diary reveals that the makeshift living conditions were far from ideal: 'The hospital had only just opened up in a field and there was a great deal of mud.' Mud was for nurses, as well as for soldiers, inevitable during their service on the Western Front. By now Violetta Thurstan's advice about the usefulness of galoshes must have rung true. 62CCS staff never discover whether McCarthy's optimism that the sisters' quarters would be 'excellent when established' was well-founded; they were soon off again, as they would be for weeks.

Respite from this frenetic activity arrived in an unwelcome form. Beatrice is one of the 166 'Sick Sisters' recorded in McCarthy's 25 August 1918 diary entry. It is easy to forget that nurses also succumbed to sickness and died of disease. The Western Front alone contains burials of over 70 British, Colonial and American nurses who lost their lives through their service.

Beatrice had developed neuralgia. Her fear of being sent back to

England and relief when she was not, was shared by other sick nursing personnel. This is one of the most gendered of wartime experiences. Wounded/ill men were desperate to get a 'Blighty ticket', yet most serving women were desperate not to. For women, this desire to avoid being repatriated may have stemmed from a twofold anxiety. Apart from dismissal, the greatest penalty for nursing personnel was to be 'returned' to England. Those who were sent back sick may have feared this being constructed by those at home as their being in some way professionally unfit for Active Service – there were also still hundreds of nurses eager to take their place.

Additionally, those who had nursed overseas would have found it ever harder to empathise with nurses who had remained at home. Home-based staff simply would not be able to understand the experiences of those who had nursed overseas – experiences which some home-based staff at least had been eager to share, but for various reasons had not been selected for overseas duty. Only those who had experienced it could fully comprehend the terror and the exhilaration of wartime service.

Such fears would have lain behind Beatrice's relief that the Sick Sisters' facilities at Château Mauricien, and subsequently Hardelot for convalescence, were her destinations. Contemporary accounts of these venues indicate that, maybe for the first time in her life, Beatrice would have been truly looked after, even cosseted. At Hardelot, nurses were encouraged to have breakfast in bed and the highly qualified chef prepared meals that made at least one nurse believe she had eaten her way back to good health. Situated near the sea front, Hardelot enabled those who were convalescing or who were close to mental breakdown to regain their strength in conducive surroundings, close to the gentle sound of the sea and away from the booming anger of the guns, which many of them had ringing in their ears on arrival.

Once recovered, Beatrice was again for team work with another flying visit to 62CCS, now at Rémy Siding. Her 'old Colonel' (Lieutenant–Colonel Marrott RAMC) was delighted to see her. 62CCS had come in for more than its fair share of bombardments, and was almost certainly overwhelmed with work. When McCarthy visited, just as Beatrice arrived, she noted that, 'the Operating Theatre was working and seemed lacking in order, and there was no Sister in either the Resuscitation or the Pre-operation Wards.' This undoubtedly explains why Beatrice's team had been requested. Generally, according to McCarthy, 62CCS staff are 'very keen and capable.' Now, however, even these sisters were at their wits' end. This is the only time in McCarthy's diary where she comes close to criticising any of the facilities where Beatrice worked.

Beatrice's longing to be in one place for more than a few days was still not destined to be fulfilled. She is almost immediately sent to 55CCS, where she felt despondent about the sisters' sleeping arrangements, as the beds 'were put into pits looking almost like graves.' McCarthy considered the accommodation 'deeply dug and sandbagged and thoroughly comfortable and safe, unless they are unfortunate enough to meet with a direct hit.' She found the staff 'satisfactory and everything was going smoothly and well.'

Perhaps Beatrice and McCarthy's views over sleeping arrangements diverge because McCarthy, quartered throughout the war in Abbeville, would not have been sleeping in a 'dug-in' bell tent which might take 'a direct hit'. Nor would she, as Beatrice now had to, re-use her hot water bottle water to wash in the next morning and boil it again at night. According to some accounts, nurses may have also used the water to make tea.

The Coming of Peace
In late October 1918, as the fighting moved further away, and despite dangers still being omnipresent, finally the end seemed to be in sight. Although Beatrice did not know it, the end of her present world and the beginning of a new one were on her horizon.

Stationed at 58CCS Tincourt, where she served for five continuous weeks, seemingly her longest duty in any one place after leaving 59GH, a fateful meeting occurred. An American doctor, Lieutenant Charles Aylen, who was serving with the RAMC, had recently arrived. A relationship slowly developed as the young nurse and doctor stole precious minutes together, she singing and he playing accompaniments on the piano, no doubt in the flickering light of the tented CCS. Every minute was precious: the war was still not over, life was fragile and might be short, as Beatrice, still sleeping in a dug-out, reminds us. And even if death spared them, either one of them was liable to be posted elsewhere at a moment's notice.

Like many, indeed most, serving personnel news of the Armistice took Beatrice by surprise. Memoirists refer to their immediate sense of shock and disbelief. For those working in hospitals, joy was tempered by the knowledge that the crippled were crippled for ever, not just 'For the Duration.' It is unsurprising that their rejoicing was tinged with despair and that some at the Front were deeply offended by what they deemed excessive jubilation and celebration back at home.

Nurses serving in France and Flanders at the end of the war quite often mention in their writings visiting the 'Forward Areas'. For more than four years, the area we now think of as 'the Western Front' had been fought over, bombed and shelled. As the opposing sides had advanced and retreated, they left in their wake destroyed towns and villages. Some citizens who had fled in 1914 found on their return after the war that their entire villages, let alone their homes, no longer existed; every building had been obliterated. When Beatrice mentions visiting what 'was Villers Carbonnel', she was not exaggerating. In May 1917, when McCarthy visited the HQ of the 4th Army, she made the point that this was now in Nissen Huts, 'Villers Carbonnel being completely devastated.'

Villers-Carbonnel is not the only village Beatrice mentioned; those she named and countless others suffered the same fate. Inevitably it was many years before they were rebuilt, with significant assistance from the American Red Cross. A number of English towns and villages also contributed to the re-building via Twinning Associations, leading to some links that remain to this day and others that have faded from memory.

In November 1918, Beatrice saw for herself the destruction that had been visited upon Belgium back in 1914 by the advancing enemy. In the riverine town of Dinant, she heard of the horrors the town endured on 23 August 1914. The inglorious tale is briefly summarised: the Germans accused the inhabitants of fighting alongside the French, and they punitively killed 674 inhabitants, approximately one in ten citizens; 1,100 buildings were destroyed and 400 men deported to German labour camps.

She also visited Louvain, which had burned for five nights from 25 August 1914. A fifth of the eleventh century town's buildings were destroyed, including the university; its fifteenth century library was razed, with its priceless books and manuscripts lost for ever, an action that caused international outrage at the time and came to symbolise the barbarism of the foe. This, like the massacres at Dinant and other Belgian towns and villages, was part of the German strategy of instilling fear and terror in the occupied population in the hope of securing civilian co-operation.

The other 'atrocity' story Beatrice hears, and which she rightly disbelieved, related to corpses being melted down in order to distil glycerine for munitions factories. *The Times* first ran the story in April 1917 and it was rapidly picked up and disseminated by the English and French-speaking press. Vehemently denied by Germany at the time but still believed by many and used as propaganda, it was finally laid to rest in December 1925 with a House of Commons statement that there had never been any foundation for the story. Truth is known to be the 'first casualty of war'. The exaggeration, or indeed fabrication of atrocity stories has been at least partly responsible for Belgium and Belgians' sufferings remaining under-researched in the Great War's historiography.

Perhaps due to a need to put the visits nurses were paying to the 'Devastated Areas' on some form of official footing, McCarthy notes on 31 January 1919 (having again given a negative response to the pesky dancing question), that she was willing for staff to visit the 'Forward Areas', as long as 'the patients were not going to suffer.' Patients' needs were always at the forefront of McCarthy's mind, as they were with the majority of nurses. A postscript to the dancing prohibition is that in the summer of 1919 the rule was again relaxed, but only for a month.

Although Beatrice rarely mentions her patients' nationalities – they are all 'our poor boys' – it seems that she nursed Indian troops after the Armistice. Over one and a quarter million Indians fought alongside the British. Of these, 77,000 died, 16,400 were wounded and 840 went missing or were taken prisoner. The wounded were cared for as compassionately and attentively as their Caucasian brothers-in-arms; comforts were provided by the Indian Soldiers' Comfort Fund, an English charity established in 1914. In a period when what we now term racism was all-pervasive, it is heartening to read that one wounded Indian wrote to his family saying, 'Do not worry about me, for I am in paradise.' When the Royal Family visited Indian troops who were nursed in the Brighton Pavilion, this same correspondent also wrote that he was proud that he had shaken the King Emperor's hand.

Another of Beatrice's post-war duties was nursing 'Self-inflicted wounds' (SIW), which a CCS at Brandhoek had specialised in throughout hostilities. During the war, a number of men wounded themselves. Some anticipated being caught but anything seemed preferable to another tour in the trenches; others hoped (and indeed no doubt a number managed) to pass these off as 'legitimate' wounds. Prior to court martial, SIW patients were generally compassionately cared for by nursing staff, with some nurses expressing sympathy for these patients. SIWs continued post-war, too. Many survivors expected to be demobbed immediately the guns fell silent. When this did not happen, some erroneously hoped that wounding themselves might hasten the process. Nursing after the Armistice remained emotionally as well as physically onerous.

Beatrice's relatively happy time at 58CCS was curtailed by her early December leave. She correctly calculated that her chances of returning were slim. Hospitals were now battling the deadly Spanish flu, which would kill more people than the war had done; the mortality rate was 20 times higher than normal influenza. It has been cited as the most devastating epidemic in recorded world history, with an estimated 20 to 40 million fatalities. Beatrice may have developed immunity to the virus through her nursing. Like many other war-weary sisters, in the summer of 1918 she had a 'touch of influenza'. Known as the 'three-day fever', this appeared without warning but, unlike the strain scourging the world from late 1918 onwards, few deaths were reported.

When the flu swept in, 'like a thief in the night', according to Medical Officer Sir George Newman, nurses were as rushed off their feet as they had been during some of the fiercest fighting. Many found failure to save those who had survived the war amongst the most heart-rending part of their service – and, of course, nurses themselves also succumbed. With no antibiotics, a population debilitated by four long years of fighting, and the majority of younger people possessing no immunity to the virus, the medical profession had nothing in its arsenal with which to fight. Even Matron McCarthy admitted after visiting 57CCS, 'there was no doubt, [*many of them*] were not going to recover. The work the nurses were doing was simply magnificent.' Although Beatrice could not have known it, the Acting Matron in charge of these 'magnificent' nurses was soon to assist in her destiny.

Despite Beatrice's regrets at being sent to a different facility, 48CCS now stationed at Namur, she was for once living in a modicum of comfort. During a June 1919 visit, McCarthy reports that 'the Hostel is a most comfortable, not to say luxurious, house, very well kept and managed.' Whether Beatrice felt as comfortable as McCarthy appears to have done about the 'young German' waiting at table in the officers' mess is impossible to know.

McCarthy also felt that Una Russell Lee QAIMNS(R) 'manages

everything splendidly'; high praise for a woman who had only been in charge of 48CCS for a month, but who had arrived with the commendation of being 'hard working, and pleasing in manner.' She was noted as having concern for the welfare of those serving under her and having her 'nurses' willing obedience'. The redoubtable Dame Maud may not have known that this splendid management and concern for welfare had recently extended to smoothing the path of one young nurse's romance. With her bitter experience of retreating under bombardment, of being shelled, working 16-hour days and now fighting the deadly influenza pandemic sweeping across Flanders, it may have seemed to Una, whose kindness and tact had been noted by her commanding officers, that it would be unfair to deny one of her nurses the opportunity of grasping love and happiness with both hands.

As spring came slowly to the peacetime world, thanks to the kindly Una, Beatrice and Charles' romance had an opportunity to blossom. They spent a whole day together in Dinant – rare when leave was counted in hours or at the most half-days, almost certainly becoming engaged, as 'the trees stirred the wind to a gentle whisper.' Yet, their chances of survival in the now flu-wracked world remained precarious. Many wartime engagements, when marriage was postponed until after the Armistice, never took place when, having both survived the war, one partner died of flu.

Beatrice's time at Namur was all too brief. Almost before she has had time to settle in, she is off once again, this time to 20CCS in Charleroi, 'an enormous building, very full both with officers and men, many critically ill,' (McCarthy). Once again, the Sister-in-charge, Sister Mary Bayne Lawson, TFNS, smoothed the way of romance. Mary had been appointed to 20CCS in December 1918. She had been on sick leave for a month due to a furnucolosis of the face caused, according to her medical reports, by 'nursing septic cases'.

Her confidential reports reveal her kindness to patients, her tact and her administrative qualities. Her kindness extended to giving Beatrice an hour's leave to spend with Charles who, having been demobbed in Germany, was passing through on his way back to England and then on to Canada. Beatrice was also allowed her two weeks' special leave. Although nursing pressures had reduced, special leave was not automatically awarded. Beatrice being granted this may be testimony to her commitment, dedication and skills.

'My boy met me at the station'

When she returned to Charleroi, Beatrice's Army Nursing Service days were drawing to a close. Many women left the Services with a heavy heart, wondering if they could ever find their way back to Civvy Street. They, their families at home, and the world they had known had all changed unutterably. Beatrice's world would change even more than most for, on 18 October 1919, she crossed the Atlantic as a 'war bride' – a term usually associated in the popular imagination with the American GI brides of the Second World War.

During the First World War, almost 13,000 Australian soldiers returned home as married or about-to-be married men; during the short time they were overseas, around 10,000 soldiers of the American Expeditionary Force married, or subsequently married, European women. Around 40,000 Englishwomen went to Canada as 'war brides'. It is easy for these numbers to simply become statistics. Each marriage was a leap of faith for the couple, many of whom could, like Beatrice and Charles, have barely known each other when they wed. It is worth noting that had Beatrice married a British soldier, she would have been forced to resign from the TFNS as, although permission to marry was granted to nurses during hostilities, married women could be TFNS nurses merely for 'The Duration'.

The Canadian Government offered free passage and arranged transport up to December 1919 for soldiers' fiancées, wives, and sometimes children. Beatrice crossed the Atlantic on designated carrier SS *Megantic*. Previously used as a troopship, the *Megantic* had been attacked by a German U-boat in 1917. Presumably, as Charles originally served with the Canadian Army Medical Services, Beatrice qualified for a passage on board – or perhaps he felt it would be easier for her to travel surrounded by others who were undertaking the same journey for a similar purpose. Aware that the initial passages had not been without hitches for the women, the Canadian Secretary of the YWCA (Sister organisation to the YMCA) came to England to assist in the transition. Beatrice may have had further cause to be grateful to the 'Y'.

As happened to many other nurses, before she left for her new life, Beatrice became entangled with army bureaucracy. Files in the National Archives detail her ever-increasing sense of desperation, as she tried to expedite payment of the salary, bonus and gratuity she was owed. Beatrice, whose pay for August and September, let alone her bonus and gratuity, had never reached her, confessed to being urgently in need of the money that she was owed. Letters and finally a telegram flew between Nottingham and London, to little avail.

Having received a personal letter from Beatrice in which she expressed a sense of despair, writing 'I cannot seem to do anything,' TFNS Matron-in-Chief Sydney Browne, entered the fray. Two days before Beatrice was due to sail, Browne reminded the Paymaster-in-Chief Eastern Command that 'this case is very urgent.' Victory finally went to the women and Beatrice left for the New World with £14 11s 3d, in cash, in her pocket.

Had she kept in touch with the kindly Mary Bayldon, Matron of 4NGH who in those distant Lincoln days had advised the recently qualified nurse to apply for overseas duties, Beatrice would have sympathised with Mary's own struggles. She too was embroiled in a battle with the War Office (Pensions). Invalided out of the service by a Medical Board in 1919, who acknowledged that her severe rheumatism and debilitating pain were a direct result of her war service and that she may never work again, Mary struggled to get the pension due to her. There may have been times in their bureaucratic battles when Beatrice and Mary felt that nursing the wounded was easier than fighting the War Office for what was rightfully theirs.

On her long journey to Canada, perhaps Beatrice re-lived memories of her service as a TFNS nurse. One surely towered above them all. On 28 June 1919, she was one of only seven nurses representing the Army Nursing Services in the Charleroi Peace Processions. Travelling in the first of the two cars carrying personnel of the ANS, accompanying the Colonel and the QAIMNS(R) Sister-in-charge, 'fever-trained' TFNS Beatrice had, through her own professionalism, skills, courage and resilience, earned her rightful place amongst the elite of the Army Nursing Service, whose members were selected from the *crème de la crème* of the officer class. As she acknowledged the cheering crowds, Nurse Beatrice Harriet Hopkinson had come a long way from the young hotel chambermaid.

Select Bibliography

Bingham, Stella, *Ministering Angels* (Osprey, 1979).

Cowen, Ruth ed., *A Nurse at the Front The First World War Diaries of Sister Edith Appleton* (Simon and Schuster, 2013).

Gliddon, Gerald, *VCs of the First World War: The Final Days 1918* (Sutton, 2004).

Purdom, C. B., 1930. *Everyman at War* (Everyman, 2000).

Moriarty, Dorothy, *Dorothy: The Memoirs of a Nurse* (Corgi, 1991 edition).

Summer, Anne, *Angels and Citizens: British Women as Military Nurses 1854-1914* (Routledge and Keegan Paul, 1988).

Thurstan, Violetta, *A Textbook of War Nursing* (George Putnam, 1917).

Wilcocks, Richard, *Stories From The War Hospital* (Meerkat, 2014).

Periodicals:

British Journal of Nursing. Available at *http://rcnarchive.rcn.org.uk*

The Monthly Record of the 4th Northern General Hospital, October 1916 – October 1917.

Stand To! and *The Bulletin,* The Western Front Association.

Primary Sources:

The National Archives: Nurses' Service Records (WO 399):

- Mary Bayldon (WO/399/9698)
- Beatrice Hopkinson (WO/399/12153)
- Mary Bayne Lawson (WO/399/12700)
- Mabel Whiffin (WO/399/15442)

Available at: *www.nationalarchives.gov.uk/records/army-nurses-service-records.htm*

Websites:

Australian War Memorial. Available at: *http://static.awm.gov.au/images/collection/pdf/RCDIG1069518—1-.PDF*

The Great War Archive, University of Oxford.
  Available at: *www.oucs.ox.ac.uk/ww1lit/gwa*

Scarlet Finders: *War Diary, Matron-in-Chief British Expeditionary Force. WO95/3988-91* (transcribed by Sue Light).
  Available at: *www.scarletfinders.co.uk*

II

Beatrice Hopkinson's War Diary, 1914–1918

'My Experiences at the Front'

—◇—

I have been asked to write my experiences while serving as a sister in the British Army. This I will endeavour to do and make it as interesting as possible, but, having no literary talent, am afraid my efforts will be in vain.

I first started my nursing career in the year 1910, at the Fever Hospital in Nottingham, England. After serving two years I passed my examinations and, winning my certificate for a fever trained nurse, I signed on for three years' general service in the County Hospital, Lincoln. It was while [*I was*] still a probationer at this hospital [*that*] the War commenced in 1914. The Government commandeered three of our wards for military use, and I was one of the probationers chosen to help look after our poor boys.

Nursing in Blighty: Lincoln, August 1914 – April 1917

I well remember the first convoy arriving. We had no ambulances and we hired a traction engine and furniture van, which were fixed up for stretcher cases. The sitting patients were taken in private cars belonging to the different townspeople. Some of the cases we received were not so bad, so they were able to go along to the bath, have hot cocoa and sandwiches, or whatever was going, and get to bed; but the worst cases we had to bathe, do their dressings and fix them up. How happy they looked in spite of their wounds. They were back again in Blighty, away from the War and that is all they cared [*about*].

I recall, we had one boy called Isit, a private. He had practically half the muscles of his back blown away by a dum-dum bullet [*A bullet with its point cut off before firing, which made a very small entrance wound but a very large exit wound. These had been banned under the 1899 Hague Conventions.*]. He was a cheery soul and would not stay in bed, but would help the more helpless boys. When they were on the way to recovery, passes out were allowed for two hours daily, and one would often see a Tommy with one arm, wheeling another Tommy in a bath chair, with a broken limb etc.

Labour at this time was very hard to get on account of the boys joining up, and the Hospital had not seen the barber for about a fortnight. Often the boys asked, "When is the barber coming, Sister?"[1] So, I determined to try, if they would let me, [*to*] shave them. Private Allen was the first and he had about a month's growth on his top lip. He told me I had shaved his face beautifully and would I try that top lip. Much encouraged by his praise, I said I would try. I had only got halfway through when he said, "I cannot stand any more, Sister." When I got to the top of the ward I heard him say, "And she said, 'Did it hurt?' God! I thought my top lip was coming off!" However, I shaved the boys often and sometimes clipped their hair. They did not seem to mind what one did.

Soon some of these boys were marked up for convalescence. It was hard to see them go, but we had to make room for the more needy cases which were ever coming in. Our next convoy was quite heavy and we had several deaths. One night about nine o'clock, one of the Tommies, very badly wounded, died. I had been frightfully busy all day, and after the night nurse came, I rushed off to evening prayers which were held in our chapel; but I seemed too tired to concentrate and as Matron uttered the prayers, I seemed to lose myself altogether, and a vision seemed to appear to me.

I saw Christ standing as though out of a cloud at the side of the Cross, wearing flowing white robes; his arm outstretched, pointing to a beautiful golden sun slowly arising out of the cloud at his feet. On the sun a scroll appeared, with the inscription, 'This I did for you – what doest –?' The rest of the sentence was hidden by the cloud. In the cloud, above Christ's head, were three Cherubims, holding a golden crown and golden rays streamed down on the scroll, making it one golden glow.

It seemed some little time before I pulled myself together and I could not forget it. In fact, the vision had been so vivid to me, I determined to try to sketch it, and send it to my brother [*who was*] serving as a sapper in the Royal Engineers in France. He was a good-living boy, and I knew he would explain it to the best of his ability. In about two weeks' time I received the reply. It was very comforting, and he believed as I did, that it must have been a vision. His explanation was very beautiful, but I cannot remember [*it*] to write it now.

It was about three weeks or a month after this that I received word that he had been killed by a stray shell;[2] a piece of shrapnel entering the jugular vein, death being almost instantaneous. I remember receiving that letter: the sun was shining so beautifully and the birds all singing. They seemed to mock me as I stood, too numb to move. My brother dead! Our dearest boy, who had been almost father and mother to us since my mother's death. Then I read again, 'We laid him very gently in his last resting place; only wrapped in a blanket, but his soul had already gone to God,' and they said he looked so peaceful.

I rushed from the ward and, without knocking, burst into our Matron's office, and exclaimed, "Matron, Matron, they have killed my brother!" Matron took me in her arms and led me up to my bedroom. Her tears flowed with mine and I said, "Matron, it is hard," and she said, "Yes, dear I know; I have already had three of my brothers killed in this War." This was a great shock to me, as no one had known and she had gone about her duties in the same way – so brave. I thought, 'I must and will be like our Matron,' and I succeeded. We had a Roll of Honour in our church in the hospital, and his name was put there, under the inscription 'For God, King and Country' and I add[*ed*] also, 'To save us'.

I have often wondered since if the vision I saw was a warning of my brother's death, with its message, 'This I did for thee, what doest thou for me?'

In July 1916, my three years at this hospital were ended. My examinations passed and with my certificates won – which I was very proud of – I left to enjoy a well-earned holiday. My Matron, who was the Principal of the Fourth Northern Military Hospital before-mentioned, asked me if I would care to join up with her unit. Having nothing definite in view, I consented, filled out the different papers and was enrolled as a Territorial Nursing Sister. After two months' holiday, I returned to Lincoln to the Fourth Northern and was put to work in Ward Two – Heavy Surgical.

There were some terrible cases, but they were all so cheery. Our ward held thirty-six patients in the top half and thirty-six in the lower. The top half was for the worst cases, and they were moved down to the lower half when they did not require so much attention. The ward was run by two Royal Army Medical Corps Orderlies, one sister in charge, two staff nurses and two VADs (Voluntary Aid Detachment). The only difference between the sister in charge and the staff nurses was that the former wore two red stripes on her arms. We staff nurses used to call them 'stripers'. We were under them and had to 'love and obey', which at times was very hard, especially so in cases where the staff nurse was older; and often the sister in charge had been a probationer under the staff nurse in her training days. I am afraid, in many cases bitter feelings raged. I was very fortunate: my sister in charge was very human and did not believe in bossing.

After a fortnight in the acute half, I was moved down to the lower half; the other staff nurse being sent on night duty, and here I was able to run things my own way, occasionally receiving advice from the head sister. They were a very happy crowd down there and used to have fine times.

We formed what we called a 'Secret Society of Seven'. One could join by paying sixpence. It was quite an event when we initiated a new member. All the different brothers and sisters were called and they all had to swear on the sign, which was a triangle with a red hand in the centre. If the chief approved, the member was given a name and ever after called by that name. Some of the names were: 'Worthy Brother One-Leg' (he only had one leg!), 'Worthy Brother Doughnut' (he used to make doughnuts! They were not a huge success but the boys thought they were grand).

I remember once the Colonel was very late, so we thought he would not be coming around. 'Worthy Brother Doughnut' thought he would like to give us a treat, so he made his 'special'. We had fried about six when in came the Colonel. Of course, everyone jumped to his bed and stood to attention. The fat was forgotten until we heard the Colonel yell, "For goodness sake have you got a gas attack on down here?" Certainly, it looked as though we had. The air was blue and most of the patients in that vicinity began to sneeze, with their eyes growing red and watery.

The Colonel was a humorous old soul and, after finding out the cause, gave the chief a sum of money, saying he would very much like to join the Society. The Colonel's wife also joined and 'Worthy Doughnut' gave her one of his doughnuts. She said in an aside to me, "Are they all right?" I convinced her they were – at least I thought I had convinced her. I found the doughnut reposing on our duty-room table afterwards.

Occasionally we used to knight our 'brothers' for any special service. We liked this, as there was always a very good supper afterwards. On one occasion we gave a rabbit supper, another pancakes. Well I remember standing frying over one hundred pancakes. I was almost a pancake myself when I had finished.

It was whilst [*we were*] frying the pancakes [*that*] the Padre came in and wanted to know all about it. He seemed quite interested, [*and*] gave us a half crown to become a member. Ever afterwards he was called 'Worthy Brother Sky Pilot'. Evidently the society had impressed him a great deal, as his sermon on Sunday consisted chiefly of this and the good spirit in the wards. The hospital boasted of a monthly magazine [*The Magazine: The Monthly Record of the 4th Northern General Hospital*]. All patients able to sketch or write were invited to contribute. One of our 'Worthies' wrote a sketch on the Secret Society of Seven, which was a great success.

I forget to mention my names [*nicknames*]; I had two. All day, until five in the evening, I was 'Worthy Sister Ray of Sunshine', but after that time, when I used to take around the medicine I was called the 'Panther of Death'. This was later explained in the magazine, as I was the only one who could give out the mystic potion successfully!

I stayed in this ward three months. By that time our secret society had grown to forty-three. Then I was told I was for night duty. The boys were sorry to lose me, but never a morning passed without some of the society coming up to see me with greetings from all. This may sound very childlike, but it kept up a good feeling and the boys did not feel their pains nearly so much.

For three months I stayed on night duty and was in charge of two hundred patients, medical and surgical. There were four huts of fifty beds each and I had one VAD in each hut. All convoys seemed to arrive during the night and this kept us very busy. Sometimes some [*patients*] would need immediate operations and the writing one had to do often took a few hours. We used to start work about three o'clock, as there were not many patients who could make their own beds, and it took quite a long time washing patients, making their beds, taking temperatures, medicines, dressings etc.

One night I went on duty and Sister reported: "Private Maxwell has had two teeth out; give him mouth washes." After the people had departed I went in to see him and said, "How is the mouth, Maxwell?" He answered, "All right, thanks, Sister," so I told him if he did not feel like getting up in the morning he could stay in bed and have a light breakfast of bread and milk. He said, "Yes Sister."

I noticed the patient slept soundly and that his mouth did not seem to worry him at all. In the morning I enquired how he was. He said, "Fine." All the other patients seemed in sympathy and asked him had he had gas or cocaine, did it hurt, etc.? He laughed; it was then I discovered he had had two teeth taken off a false plate because they were loose!

Soon after this I was taken off night duty, and I was not sorry as I had had a very hard time with several deaths. It was terrible to see some of the boys' wounds – but oh, they were so brave with all their sufferings. Nothing seemed to matter as long as they were in Blighty. Often Tommies with very severe wounds and double amputations would say, "Didn't I get a nice Blighty, Sister?" (Meaning a wound that would take them home to England.)

I was sent to the Fracture Ward. Almost all of the patients were on Balkan beams. (A beam standing on trestles over the patient's bed, very strongly made so [*that*] movement would not jar the patient). The leg or arm would be put up in a 'Thomas' splint and swung on pulleys to the beam, so that the patient could move up and down without hurting the limb. We had some very interesting work here. Our Major in charge of the ward was very clever and very cynical. He often would ask extraordinary things, and unless you had worked with him some little time, he was very hard to understand. We had a new staff nurse one day, and he said to her, "Sister, give me a knife and fork." [*The*] poor Sister immediately went into the kitchen and brought him a knife and fork; he meant forceps and scalpel!

April – July 1917

It was while [*I was*] working in this ward that I heard I was for Foreign Service; so Matron thought I might take my leave, which was then due. I packed and was soon on my way, but I had only been home five days when I received a telegram ordering my return without delay. I packed quickly and caught the next train and, taking a taxi at the station, was soon up at the Fourth Northern in the presence of our Matron. She informed me that orders had come through for us to 'Stand To' until further orders.

Next morning, we all, the twenty of us that were going, went down to the operating theatre and received our first inoculation of the anti-typhoid serum. The inoculation was not at all bad but the after effects were terrible. I was running a temperature of 103 and having 'rigors' all afternoon. I was off-duty in the evening so I went to bed. Next morning I was feeling better, but my arm was very painful and it was very difficult to do my hair. Most of the other sisters were the same and we sympathised, one with the other. The second dose was not so bad.

For weeks we waited, but nothing happened, so our Matron thought [*that those of us*] who had been recalled from holidays might try again; so, away we went, but we had only been gone three days this time when orders came through for our return. We did not worry about catching the first train this time, but waited until the last. On arriving, we were told we had again to 'Stand To'. We waited a few more weeks, and then, on the evening of 12th July 1917, we were told our final orders were through and we had to report to our principal matron at the Country Hospital.

I was off in the evening, so got all my packing done and then waited for my chums to come off-duty. They came about nine o'clock. They were so excited, and said, "We are going to have a last flare!" Each proceeded to find what eatables she had. One brought doughnuts, another cake, another biscuits, another chocolates which we all looked very longingly at. Another sister brought egg sandwiches. We looked when we saw these and many exclaimed "Where did you get the bread and butter?" She explained it was her ration she had used up and we would have to provide her with the 'staff of life' for the next few days.

We were all rationed and for weeks had carried our own bread, butter, jam and sugar, backwards and forwards to the hospital. We saw that she was all right and had plenty to eat until she received her next loaf. We kept the party up until 2 a.m., even then we did not feel at all sleepy and it was some little time before we finally settled down.

Interlude: From London to France, July 1917
The next morning we reported to our principal [*matron*], signed heaps of papers, also received two months' salary in advance. We were informed that the ambulance would be at the hostel at 10 a.m. That meant we had to hurry, as we all had several little things we had to do. Promptly at ten the ambulance arrived. As many jumped in as possible and off to the station we went.

At 10.20 a.m. the train came streaming in, goodbyes were said; promises to write given and snaps taken of us as the train steamed out of the station. Soon after 2 p.m. we arrived in London and were soon on our way in taxis to the Berners and York Hotels, where we were to find our matron in charge of the party.

After engaging our rooms and getting our luggage to them, we walked over to the York Hotel to report our arrival to the matron.[3] We were told to go downstairs to the lounge. We were all discussing what was in store for us; where the matron was and what was she like. We eventually found the room and heard a cheery voice saying, "Come right in, all of you." I have often thought since, that Matron must have been much amused at overhearing our remarks about her. We entered to find a most cheery-faced little woman. She asked us where we had come from and we informed her: the Fourth Northern General at Lincoln.

Names and ranks were taken of all and we were told to report again in about two hours' time. This we did, to find the room packed with Territorial Sisters and VADs from Leicester, Sheffield, Leeds and Newcastle, making a total of ninety-three. Matron informed us that she had received orders from our chief at the War Office,[4] and we were to continue our journey on the morrow. The rest of the day was our own; she would tell us the time of departure in the morning, when the sister in charge of each unit was to report at 10 a.m. to receive instructions.

We went up to the top lounge, but did not stay there very long as the place was packed. I have often wished since that I could paint, so that I could put on canvas the picture we saw. Sisters in uniform, it seemed, of almost every country: Britain, Canada, South Africa, Australia, New Zealand and America. Some were in their mess dresses with their white caps; others in out-door uniform, all awaiting orders. Mingled here and there with these women of mercy, were other women in civilian dress, smoking and drinking tea etc., some entertaining officers, their khaki helping in the colour of the picture. Some of these women looked enviously at us, whilst others seemed that a good time in life was all they wanted. What did they care if our country was at war, so long as they got the enjoyment they craved? I pitied them, the poor aimless butterflies.

I think during the evening almost all of us went to a theatre of some place of amusement, as we did not know when we should see another good play. Next morning we awaited the return of our sister in charge. She returned about eleven and told us that we were to leave London for

Folkestone from Charing Cross Station at two o'clock; and that we were to be punctually at the station, with our luggage in order, at one-thirty p.m.

Immediately after lunch we hired taxis and drove to Charing Cross Station, got our luggage insured and everything in order. Soon the gates were opened leading down to the Staff Train. Having our passes and embarkation tickets in order, we were allowed to pass through and secured a very nice carriage for six of us. Just before the whistle sounded for the train to move on, our Matron-in-Chief, from the War Office, came along the platform and wished us all a pleasant voyage and told us to do our best, as we were greatly needed by our boys in France.

The whistle sounded and the train began to move slowly out of the station. We waved our handkerchiefs to our Matron-in-Chief, and some to their friends who had come to see them off. How that train travelled, with never a stop and how hot we got, all longing for a good cup of tea. Suddenly I bethought myself, I had my Tommy's cooker in my case, with condensed milk and sugar. We secured water on the train and made tea for the six in our compartment. It was tedious work, as the pan only held sufficient for one cup of tea and we had to keep water boiling for each. I was very glad when I could sit down with mine, which I thoroughly enjoyed. It was the last good cup of tea we were to have for several days.

About five or six p.m. we reached Folkestone. The sun was shining beautifully and promised a smooth crossing as the sea was almost as still as a mill-pond. Soon we were on the boat, the *Victoria*. From the deck we watched two other boats which were embarking Tommies. These pulled out to sea ten or fifteen minutes before us. We too had quite a number of Tommies and officers on board. Soon our boat was ready and the siren sounded, and we began to slowly pull out. It was not long before we were in the open sea, with destroyers around us and an aeroplane circling above with its every watchful observer on the lookout for lurking submarines.

It was a beautiful crossing and I think we all enjoyed it as we marched backward and forwards along the deck, with our life-saving jackets on; two thoughts uppermost in our minds – were we going to be torpedoed or sea-sick? But we were neither.

St. Omer, France: July 1917 – September 1917

The evening sun was glorious as we entered Boulogne Port. Everywhere on the quay seemed very busy; orders were shouted to several officers on board – where to report etc., through a megaphone by a sergeant. We also received instructions to stay on board until the last. Then we all lined up on the quay with the embarkation sister, who met us, in charge. After our luggage was taken off and instructions given as to our destinations; we were arranged into three groups, to go to different places for the night. The Hostel Hotel du Nord and Hotel Louv[r]e. Our party was to stay at the Louv[r]e.

Well I remember our walk up to this hotel and my first impressions of France were not very good. There was a strong smell of fish everywhere. The roads were very dirty and the noise was terrific. Hooters and whistles, and the clanging of machinery intermingled with the cries of the people; columns of khaki-clad boys marching to the various camps around helping in the noise. We found ourselves almost shouting in one anothers' ears to make ourselves heard.

The Hotel Louv[r]e was not very far from the quay and stood facing the Hotel Crystal across the quay. We entered and were told to wait in the sitting room for further orders. How that place smelled of stale tobacco, food and a musty smell, as though the place had been closed for years; owing to the absence of fresh air, I suppose. It seemed to me that the French people didn't seem to like fresh air. I fancy, too, they thought we were very strange people for wanting our bedroom windows open, for as fast as we opened them, they closed them again.

In a little while, the embarkation sister returned. After taking our names, rank and unit, she told us we might go to dinner. The food was good, but cooked differently to what we were used to and there seemed to be no shortage of anything. The butter was good. We'd had nothing but margarine for almost a year in England, so the change was very welcome.

It was about nine p.m. when dinner was over and we were able to retire to our rooms. We were all very tired and looked forward to a good hot bath and a night's sleep before continuing our journey on the morrow. Imagine our disappointment when we found we were to get neither. We searched all over the hotel for bathrooms and the only one we could find had a bed made up in it with someone sleeping there. We saw an officer in khaki coming out in the morning. Everywhere was so congested they had to put them to sleep in any available space. I was told afterwards that every spot in the corridors, sitting-rooms and lounges were used for the same purpose. No wonder that place smelt so stuffy!

We gave up the bath idea and went to bed; five in one room and all as tired as tired could be; but sleep never came. Our room faced the main street and the cries and noises we'd heard on our arrival continued all night. At 2 a.m. we gave up the idea and had a good talk, whilst watching the people and the traffic from our window. At 8.30 a.m. breakfast was served; coffee, brown bread and butter and fresh eggs. We thoroughly enjoyed that meal; we were so hungry after being awake all night. [*At*] 10 a.m. we again reported to the embarkation sister and were told we were to catch the 2 p.m. train; if any [*nurses*] were absent at that time they would be sent back to England.

We decided to spend the time looking around Boulogne. The *patisserie* (pastry) shops looked so good with their rich icings – things we had almost forgotten. I think nearly all the sisters sampled these cakes and bought more for the train journey.

We saw the casino, then being used as a hospital, a very beautiful place standing near the sea. The streets we found very difficult to walk upon, as they were all cobbled and some very narrow. The tide was coming in very quickly and with it the fishing boats. Some were already unloading their catch. We were very interested as we watched. After unloading, the fish was wheeled on barrows into the fish market, so we followed. Here we saw very old women, with faces yellow and wrinkled like parchment, their shoulders bent over, wearing snowy white caps, sitting with their bare feet in the baskets of fish, with eels still wriggling about the place. These women were all talking together and they sounded so strange to us. All we seemed to make out if it was, "Yar, yar…jamie, jamie"! We laughed heartily at them, and they at us, as we tried to question them.

We then went up to the Notre Dame Cathedral, but the time was getting very short so we had to beat a hasty retreat. After dinner we settled our bills and made for the station. Some of the other sisters were already there and, thank goodness, some of our boys were also there to put us on the right train. They told us our luggage was already on board and that the train did not leave until 2.30 p.m. We managed to find a nice carriage and settled ourselves to wait.

Our Matron soon came along and told us we were going to a place called St. Omer – to the 59th General Hospital, just opening in that town; and that all the ninety-three sisters and VADs were to be her staff for that hospital. We were delighted as she had been so kind to us on our journey. Matron could speak French fluently, so we had no further difficulty travelling.

The train steamed out of the station at 2.30 p.m. I believe that was one of the longest journeys I made in France by train. It seemed endless. It appeared if a hen, pig or goat got on to the line, the train gave a shriek and pulled up. This happened frequently.

The scenery was beautiful and the day glorious but unbearably hot. How we wished the journey would come to an end. Two or three freight trains passed us, filled with Tommies going on leave. Each van had marked on it '*Hommes 40 – Chevaux 8*'. The Tommies were sitting on the tops of the vans and out on the steps; most of them singing [*such*] favourite songs as 'Take me Back to Dear Old Blighty' or 'It's a Long, Long Way to Tipperary'. They all cheered and greeted us as we passed and enquired as to where we were going.

About 7 or 7.30 p.m. we reached St. Omer. The colonel and officers, with some of the RAMC (Royal Army Medical Corps) met us. We met men from our own home unit. They were just longing for news from Blighty. Most of us had brought papers from England and these they took eagerly.

Ambulances were awaiting our arrival outside the station. These we boarded. The Colonel told us we need not worry about our luggage, as the men would see to it. In a few minutes we reached the place we were to billet – an old school – Ecole St. Marguerite in the Place St. Marguerite. This place was really intended for a section of the 59th General Hospital and beds were already made up and equipment given out. We were to stay there until we found another billet.

What a scramble there was when Matron told us we might choose our own sleeping place. There were about eight beds in the room we chose and we had to pass through another room holding about eight or nine beds. The sisters from Leicester got this and we christened it the 'Leicester Lounge' and ours 'The Lincoln Buffet'! We then went into supper. The boys had prepared quite a nice supper for us in a room across the courtyard. It almost had the appearance of a barn. We all ate very heartily of the Irish stew, rice pudding, cheese biscuits and margarine. They must have worked very hard for us and we certainly appreciated it.

After supper we had to claim our luggage, which had arrived and was stacked up in the courtyard. How I pitied those poor boys with the luggage of ninety-three people arriving in one lot; we had quite a lot each; a kit-bag holding bed, canvas bath and basin, chair – everything for camp life – cabin trunk, holdall and small handcases. But they seemed so pleased to see us that I don't think they minded how much luggage there was.

We were all very pleased to retire to our rooms; but we had not long been in bed when we heard the clanging of a big bell. The sergeant in charge of the Ecole St. Marguerite came around shouting, "All lights out – all lights out!" Then we understood we were in for an air raid. However, we were used to warnings like that in Lincoln and they'd never done any damage, so we stayed in our beds. We saw the searchlight playing and heard our anti-aircraft barrage. They were extremely close and dropped Verey lights from their planes; but we didn't hear any bombs that night and slept very soundly, only waking at 7 a.m. the next morning, which was Sunday.

It was a beautiful, bright, clear day and Matron told us all to make out a paper with our name, rank, age, religion and how long [*we had been*] in the service; when last vaccinated and inoculated; training school and qualifications. This we did and gave them in as soon as possible. After 10 a.m. we were told that the Padre would address us in the courtyard, so we assembled there. His talk was on how to address our mail and the importance of not giving secrets away. He informed us that all our letters would be censored and franked by him, and anything in the nature of names of places where we were would be scratched out. No idea was to be given as to how near or how far we were from the firing line, or even mention of the air raids.

There was a grunt of disapproval from many and cries of, "Well, but what are we to write about?" This was soon silenced by our Padre, who told us that absolute secrecy was necessary as we were in the lines of communication and anything given away might mean not only danger to us, but to the troops ever passing through the town. He pointed out that letters had often gone astray by the aid of spies who were ever about.

After this address we went over to the hospital, which was about five or ten minutes' walk from the Ecole St. Marguerite, in the Rue St. Bertin. It was a huge stone building, built by the English Jesuits years ago. The buildings formed a square, with the usual courtyard in the centre. Very tall trees surrounded the courtyard and there were small rose gardens running at intervals all around the court, making a very pretty spot. The roses were in full bloom and looked so sweet.

We entered the hospital and had a good look around. The personnel had been very busy as almost all the beds were made up. The wards were very spacious and held from seventy-three to eighty beds each. On the right side of the hospital were six wards. They had been thoroughly cleaned and whitewashed by the British. At intervals throughout the length of the ward were huge, square oaken posts extending from the floor to the ceiling. In these posts were oblong notches. These, we were told, were where the French soldiers used to swing their beds! The hospital had been a French Military Hospital before the British took it over. We hated those posts on night duty, as the bats, which were very thick around the hospital, used to hide in the notches in the daytime and appear at dusk. They were terrible things and gave us many a scare.

The front part of the hospital was used for officers and there was also an operating theatre there. The left side was used by the personnel; the barber's shop; officers' quarters; baths and isolation cases, whilst the back part of the hospital was used for stores, kitchen etc. There were some wonderful underground cellars. These were used during air raids and were fitted up with stoves, forms and rugs.

After dinner Matron told us we might all be off-duty, as there were no patients; so we went to explore the town. St. Omer is a very ancient town, with some wonderful buildings. The streets are not really as wide as town streets usually are and they are all cobbled. We noticed what a quantity of *estaminets* (beer houses) there were. It almost seemed every other door [*was an estaminet*]. These were packed with khaki boys and weird music was pouring out of every door. We found out afterwards that a penny was needed to set the machine in motion. It was of the barrel-organ type.

The floor of the *estaminet* was covered with sand. We noticed this, too, in almost all the poorer houses. It was very strange to see their method of washing their floors. They just sweep up the sand, throw a bucket of water on the floor, then sweep it out of the door. Afterwards they take a cloth, spread it out on the floor and drag it by the two corners the length of the floor, mopping up the water in this way. Afterwards more sand was thrown on the floor and that completed the process.

Here, too, we noticed the dirty condition of the streets; small and large piles of refuse standing at each door. It was not hard to guess each day what they'd had for dinner, as all the refuse would be thrown on this heap. Outside a café, one would see hundreds of egg-shells on these heaps. The Tommies were very fond of eggs and one could see if the trade had been good or bad by how much refuse there was. We were told that each heap was collected in the early morning by the dustman; but labour was very short on account of the war and that was the reason of [*sic*] the dirty appearance.

The Cathedral of St. Omer was a magnificent old building and we delighted in roaming over it. It had some beautiful paintings and carvings; a wonderful organ and crucifix, but everywhere had the same old musty smell that we had noticed in Boulogne.

It was very strange to us to be able to go into any of their churches at any time during the day. They seemed always to be open and someone always there praying, with their rosaries in hand. After wandering through the Cathedral, we went into the public garden, a nice quiet spot with beautiful flowers. The band was playing in the band-stand (one of our regimental bands) and we stayed to listen. They played every Sunday afternoon between two and four p.m. and the French, as well as the English, flocked to hear it. We spent many a pleasant hour here. Afterwards we went to Divine Service; so ended our first day in St. Omer.

The next day dawned beautifully clear and we all went on duty. Matron had placed us in the wards we were to work in, so we spent a very busy morning equipping the wards. In the afternoon we were off-duty and a number of us went into a café to see if we could get a good cup of tea; we were just longing for one. The tea came lukewarm, with the tea [*leaves*] floating on the top. We tried to explain how to make it, but the poor French mademoiselle looked so frightened. I remember one of our sisters who could speak just a little French, going into the shop and just shouting at the girl. Evidently she thought if she shouted, the girl would understand better. How we all laughed to hear her trying to explain in broken French and English. "*Thé Compre*" must be made with boiling water – *compre* boiling water; *compre l'eau* boiling; and then, "*l'eau chaud.*" I am sure that the girl thought we were all mental.

For about a fortnight we passed our time fixing our wards and exploring, in our off-duty [*time*], the town and small villages surrounding it. Some of our sisters had been sent up to Casualty Clearing Stations (a hospital next to a Field Ambulance, the nearest place to the front line a sister was allowed; we were the only females allowed so close to the line). Others had been sent to staff our other section at Moulle,[5] a village about eight or ten kilometres outside St. Omer; so that our staff of 59 General had become much smaller than we originally were.

Patients began to arrive in ones and twos from the various companies billeted around. We began to wonder when we would receive the real battle casualties, but we did not have to wait very long. About midnight one night in August, we were all roused out of our sleep and told to dress as quickly as possible and report to our wards at the hospital. We had only just got there when wounded started to pour in, and soon we had four or five of the biggest wards full.

They were patients from the New Zealand Hospital at Hazebrouck and had been shelled out by the Germans. Thank goodness they had gotten them all away without any casualties. They were a fine set of men but some had very serious wounds. Some were not in a fit condition to move, but if they had been left there they would have been killed. They had to be given some chance, but it made us very sad when the worst cases died.

About three a.m. we were able to return to our billet and bed, but we were so excited all we could do was to talk about our patients – our first real patients in France!

Next day we had orders to make room for the sisters of the New Zealand Hospital; and about dinner time they arrived. Five were put into my room, as all the other sisters had either gone on night duty to Moulle or a Casualty Clearing Station. I was very pleased to have them with me and it was not very long until we were great pals. One of the sisters had lost her brother; poor girl, my heart bled for her. She was trying to be so brave and I knew just how she felt.

Invitations began to pour in from the various Units around, for sports and concerts, etc.; well I remember our first invitation. Matron told us to put our names down, those who would like to go. I think about twenty of us went. It was on a Saturday and a glorious day. We were told the conveyance would be at the hospital door about one p.m. Imagine our surprise to find one of the old London omnibuses awaiting us. All the glass windows had been broken and pieces of wood nailed across, making the inside of the bus very dark. However, we got on top. Some of the seats had disappeared but there were heaps of empty petrol tins, which we sat on. We thoroughly enjoyed the drive as the country was looking so beautiful. It was a hot day but the movement through the air kept us cool and we were all well shaded from the sun's glare by the tall trees.

In France the trees are wonderful. One can go for miles on a road which is just one long avenue of trees. All the dense foliage is cut away at the bottom, allowing the air to get through, therefore keeping the road much cooler. These trees [*Lombardy Poplars*] are very high and their foliage meets over the road, sheltering it from the sun's rays. The country was very flat and open. It was always a marvel to me how each man guessed his own field, as they all ran into each other. The land was well cultivated. There seemed to be no waste land at all. It was wonderful to see the people of France working in the fields. The whole family would turn out at dawn and work away until dusk, with absolutely no idea of time. They would just work all day.

About three p.m. we arrived at the sports ground, and seats and programmes were provided. The sports were very good and about half-way through we were given tea. After tea we were told there was a race for us and would those who wished to compete put their names down on the paper provided. Quite a few of us entered. It was a 100 yard flat race. We got in line, the pistol was fired, and away we ran. That piece of white tape seemed so far away. I heard cries of "Come on Tiny," and on I came! I just had my hand on the tape when over I went. I was picked up by someone who said, "What is your name?" Followed by, "You are first." I was given a very useful address book as first prize.

After that we had a sack race. That was great fun as everyone fell over! Some managed to scramble to their feet, whilst others had to be liberated. A VAD came in first, and I second. It was soon time for us to depart and we boarded our bus. Good-byes and promises to come to our 'At Homes', which we held every Sunday afternoon, were given and then we were on our way.

The boys thoroughly enjoyed coming to our 'At Homes'. Our Matron was just lovely to them. They were invited to play, sing or recite. Often they told us it was like being at home again. This was the only way we could entertain our friends. We had our rules, which were very strict. We were not allowed out with any male in uniform and as we were always in uniform, mufti not being allowed on Active Service, it was very hard on us if we met, by chance, any relative or friends from home. We were just to greet them and ask them to come down to our billet, where we could meet them properly.

In September my turn came for night duty. By this time we had our new billet: General Petain's house on the Rue de'Tain, just at the back of our hospital, so that we had a very little way to go before we were on duty. It was a very nice house and had been used by the French General as a mobilizing centre for the French. He was then away with his troops, so no longer needed the house and had kindly consented to rent it to the English sisters. We had a lovely garden and spent many happy hours there.

We were kept very busy in the wards these days, as we used to receive patients from the ambulance trains passing through St. Omer, who were too ill for further journey. Some of these cases we pulled through, but mostly all died.

One poor boy we received one day was unconscious. He had a history of lying out in No-Man's Land for several days. He was in a terrible state. When we took his dressings down for the doctor to see his wounds, we found he had double fractured femur compound. He was operated on and they found his wounds full of maggots. He only lived two days, poor lad; that was only one of the many cases we had.

'Dabbling in a Sea of Blood': September 1917 – February 1918

My experience on night duty, I shall never forget. Jerry (enemy aeroplanes) had been giving us one or two scares, but nothing had definitely happened until the moon was almost full. It was what we called the 'harvest moon'. We had only just come on night duty when the whistle shrieked shrilly through the air in the courtyard below – one, two, three. Immediately all lights were put out. The bell on the ruins of the Eglise St. Bertin started its mournful tolling and the air was filled with strange noises. (The Eglise St. Bertin was an old ruined church, used as an observation post. We often saw the sentry come out of his box with his rifle in hand.)

Suddenly we heard a noise of many planes whirring through the air. Our anti-aircraft started their barrage and the searchlights were in full play. Once I saw a plane in the searchlight, with shrapnel bursting all around. The moon was riding high in the heavens, and the plane seemed as though it was making straight for the moon. Then, suddenly – bang! bang! bang! Five bombs had been dropped. Then we heard the machine gun fire from the planes at a very close range. We wondered when our turn would come.

The anti-aircraft kept up a constant barrage and the noise was tremendous. In about a half an hour's time all was quiet again and my patients soon fell asleep: but not for long. We were just beginning to think they had gone for good when we heard the bell on the St Bertin Church tolling again and before it had finished, several bombs had fallen. We could not count how many as the noise was terrific. It seemed everything was happening at once, and they were much nearer this time.

About ten or eleven p.m. there was quiet again and Matron came in, along with our tin-hatted Sergeant Major. (He always wore his tin hat on air raid nights.) She told us the last lot of bombs had been dropped on the 58th General Scottish Hospital, near the public gardens. She said they were not sure how many casualties there were, but we had to prepare to receive the patients.

My ward held seventy-three patients and was next to the operating theatre, so they filled it first. We soon had the beds turned down; mackintoshes and hot bottles in them, and waited. All this had to be done in the darkness, as the all-clear had not been sounded. Soon we heard the cars arriving and the stretcher bearers stumbling upstairs with their burdens. We threw open our doors and guided them to the nearest beds.

The first patient to arrive on a stretcher was unrecognisable as a human being and we knew there was no hope for this poor soul, so we covered him up to concentrate on the other arrivals. We soon had the ward full. Then commenced the inoculator and sorting patients out: those who needed immediate operations. How we worked that night – I will never forget. Jerry had started again outside and he kept it up until three-thirty a.m. but we were too busy to take heed. There were so many patients who were dangerously ill; they were haemorrhaging from all their wounds and it was very difficult working in the darkness.

One case had been hit on the head and his moans were terrible. He was too ill to operate on and almost pulse-less. We worked hard on this man, but he died in the early morning. I had been so busy with this poor fellow, trying to pull him through; I almost let two others slip away. They had been too ill to call and were haemorrhaging very badly. We gave them salines and stimulants and soon they were feeling a little better and their pulses much improved.

Order reigned for a little while in the ward, so that gave us a chance to tidy up. We had to cut off the patients' clothing as their wounds were so bad; and this we gathered up and stacked against the door in a huge pile. The orderly and I started to wash out the sheets and bedding in a big bath tub. Soon we seemed to be dabbling in a sea of blood. When the lights were allowed on we looked at one another and we, too, looked as though we had been in a slaughterhouse. Our clothing was blood stained up to our chins; arms and faces too.

Matron came in and put her hand on my shoulders and said, "Sister you have done very well." I almost sobbed – it seemed that kindness was all that was needed to make me break down. Those poor fellows – some of them were to have gone back to their units on the morrow, and there they lay; one poor boy with both feet off, another with an arm and leg, and so on; not one mild wound amongst them.

We soon began to feel faint for food, as we had eaten nothing all night. After a little refreshment we felt much better and it was not long before the day people came in to relieve me. What a sight met their eyes. As much as we had worked, there was still plenty to do; blood everywhere and the patients so ill they needed a lot of attention.

None of the night sisters felt they could go to bed and sleep; the horrors of the night were still with us and we felt we must see the hospital they had bombed, so we went out. The 58th Scottish Hospital was all under canvas and very near the park, as I have before mentioned; so we decided to walk through the park. We arrived there to find the place crowded with people. French gendarmes were everywhere.

We saw two orderlies approaching from the hospital, carrying a sheet. They stooped over bunches of twigs in various places and picked up something, putting it into the sheet. They were the arms and legs and other pieces of the patients that had been bombed and blown right out into the park. Oh, it was horrible, and still we could not tear ourselves away! We noticed five big bomb holes all around the bandstand and the trees had been blown off halfway, as though a big saw had been at work. Ten bombs must have fallen in the park alone.

On our way out of the park we passed the hospital. One line of marquees had absolutely been wiped out. The canvas, bedding and other equipment was hanging on trees or on the other marquees, where they had been blown by the explosion. Beds were twisted into almost unrecognizable shapes. It was a terrible mess. We spoke to one of the sisters of the hospital and she told us, as far as they could gather, over fifty patients had been killed; about one hundred wounded and some they could not find at all; also that four sisters and three VADs had been killed.

A little further along from the hospital was a German prisoner-of-war camp. We were talking to one of the sentries and he told us they had had an awful time with the prisoners. He said (I'll use his expression), "They had all been as windy (frightened) as possible." We heard afterwards from the sisters of the 58th Hospital that the prisoners were feeling terrible about the sisters and the VADs being killed, and had requested that two weeks' pay be stopped, so they might buy flowers to show their sorrow. Whether this was allowed or not, I do not know.

We finally tore ourselves away from the scene of destruction and horror, and made for our billet, but we slept very little that day. The night with its horrors would remain and Jerry came over once or twice, trying to take photographs, and our guns would start a barrage, making sleep impossible. We always knew if he came over in the daytime he would again appear at night.

When we went on duty that night, the moon was shining gloriously. How we hated the moon those days! I think we all thought we would never, never get sentimental over it again; but after war and all danger are past, the moon comes back into her own and we are just as romantic as ever; at least, I have found it so.

We had only been on duty a few minutes when the whistle blew its warning. 'All lights out!' I rushed around the ward, opened up the windows and placed the pillows of the patients nearest the windows just resting at the top of their heads, so they could pull them over their faces in case of bombs falling and breaking glass. This was a necessary precaution to prevent wounds being caused from flying glass if a bomb exploded nearby.

After this we used to go and have a chat with all the boys in turn, to give them courage. The first thing they asked for during an air raid was a cigarette. We used to strike a match under the bedclothes and light the cigarette, taking a lit one to each patient who wanted to smoke. One or two of the patients from the bombing the night before were very ill. In fact, we did not expect them to live. Several had been operated on during the day and were not feeling at all well. Poor lads, we felt so sorry for them, lying there so helpless, expecting every moment to be their last.

I was just attending to one poor fellow who had had his spleen removed earlier that day, when we heard Jerry with his first bomb. He dropped quite a number outside the town and then all was quiet again. They used to come in relays and it was not long before we had another lot, this time in the town. The patient I was attending, although in a semi-conscious state said, "Bomb! Bomb! Bomb! Don't leave me Sister; don't leave; stay with me," and again, "Bomb, bomb, bomb," as each one fell. I said, "I won't leave you, old chap; I'll stay right with you," and took hold of his hand, but I had the sense to move away from the window!

We heard a terrible noise, machine guns firing rapidly and bombs dropping; each one getting closer. I counted, "One, two, three, four, five" – the fourth one was dropped in our courtyard at the back of the hospital.

It seemed that the hospital itself was shaken on its foundations. Every door and window opened and shut, and everything shook. How we prayed that night. Our very lives depended on it. We all thought it was our last moment, but when we heard the fifth one fall, we knew we were safe for the present.

It was always a marvel to us that those two bombs should fall in that narrow space. The fifth one had fallen in a shed in the yard but had not exploded. It was a dud, which was afterwards dug up and examined by an expert on bombs. He told us it was an aerial torpedo and if the two had exploded together that side of the hospital would have been blown to pieces. If the aviator had thought one second sooner of dropping those bombs our hospital would have been wiped out. It seemed to us the hand of Providence.

I went around the ward afterwards to see if any of my patients had been hurt, as all the glass in the windows had been blown out. They were still lying with their faces covered with their pillows, and glass everywhere. Not one had a scratch, for which I was very thankful. The boys had been very quiet during the raid. All but two had remained in their beds. These two came sheepishly back after the raid, Poor lads; when I missed them, I sent [*an*] orderly with dressing gowns and slippers, as they were only in night attire and I was afraid they might get cold.

The shock of the air raid had been too much for my splenectomy boy. He died at dawn.

We soon began to hear where the bombs had fallen. Our Section 2, the Ecole St. Marguerite (which I have before mentioned as our first billet and which we were at that time using for convalescent patients), had had two bombs right on the main part of the hospital. Fortunately, the sister and doctor in charge had given orders for the patients to dress and go across the yard to the cellars. If that precaution had not been taken, everyone would have been killed. The place was one ruin afterwards, and the trees and bandstand were destroyed. One RAMC boy, who stayed at his post by the telephone, was severely wounded and brought over to the main hospital section, but he died soon after admission.

The sister in charge of Section 2 was afterwards decorated with the RRC (Royal Red Cross) and the VAD, a Canadian girl, was mentioned in dispatches.

They did not return again that night. Our anti-aircraft put up such a barrage every time they attempted that they were afraid. We were very pleased when daylight at last dawned and the sun arose in the heavens, blinking with his glorious rays everywhere. The world then seemed so peaceful and the night with its horrors almost faded away.

We did not go to the scene of the destruction this time, but went quietly to bed, thoroughly tired out with our strenuous duties of the night. Everything was quiet during the day and we slept well, but we all got up feeling that if Jerry came that night, we could not stand him any more.

When we went on duty, the patients were very quiet and mostly sleeping, tired out with so many wakeful nights. We were just sitting at our supper when the warning went again. Immediately all lights were put out, windows opened, pillows placed in position and screens put around the fireplace. We brought our supper into the ward behind the screen, against the fire, and managed to finish it by the fire's tender glow. The patients slept on and we waited, but nothing happened. This time it was not our night.

I do not know why, but that night I felt more nervous than other nights. My knees just shook and, had I allowed it, my teeth would have rattled; but I had to be brave for my patients' sake. When they saw the womenfolk apparently without fear it kept them brave.

I never realized what the word 'duty' meant until this War. To stand at one's post, never flinching and trying to keep the boys cheerful; all the time wondering when our time would come. I remember well one Scottish boy from the Tank Corp. He had been hit with a piece of shrapnel in the jugular vein. Matron came around, as she always did during air raids, to have a chat with us and try to keep our spirits up. Jock said to Matron, "Why don't you send all these women into the cellars, this is no place for them?"

Matron answered: "Jock, every one of my sisters prefers to stay with their boys. They have the privilege of going down to the cellars if they feel at all nervous, but I don't suppose Sister would go down if I told her to. Would you, Sister?"

"Certainly not. My duty is here," I replied. I moved away, but I heard Jock say to Matron what a fine set of women we were and we put some of the boys to shame.

Peace reigned for several nights. Although we had the warning, nothing happened, then on Sunday night we night people were all awakened by the hum-hum of Jerry's machines. It was about six p.m. They had been on the look-out and had seen our planes signalling on their return journey to the aerodromes. The signals used were red and white Verey lights.[6] These they copied and entered the town. Several bombs were dropped before our anti-aircraft people realized they were enemy machines. We grabbed our clothes and tore down to the cellar in our night attire. Jerry did not stay long and they were the only bombs he dropped. We were soon able to return to our rooms to dress for duty. He did not return again that evening.

We heard afterwards that he had been trying for the locks on the canal, as this would help flood the town and so prevent the constant traffic from going through. He got very near to the locks, and also bombed several French houses, killing civilians and the Tommies billeted there.

The moon by this time was on the wane and we had a little peace from the bombing. How we longed for rain during the next full moon, so it would keep Jerry away and give us a rest. Rain we had almost every night, too! We were so thankful and everyday dawned beautifully clear, enabling us to go for long tramps in the morning or 'lorry-hopping' to visit the nearest village. Lorry-hopping was stopping the first lorry that came along and asking the driver where he was going. If a reasonable distance, we boarded and went with them! We used to call them joy rides and in this way we saw a great deal of the surrounding country. One very pretty spot near St. Omer we often visited was called Clarmaris. The French people called it the 'Venice of France' and truly it answered to that name.

We often took a punt, but we also had a set of oars so we could row, as we were not used to punting. Six of us would usually go and we could keep the punt all day if we liked for the sum of one franc. These punts were very light, tapering at both ends, and the slightest movement caused them to move very quickly. Fortunately the oars were fixed on pins, on which they used to rotate.

I remember our first trip to this pretty spot. I had the oars for a short time and, not being used to them, I sent the boat in a zig-zag fashion all the way down the stream, hitting the sides of the bank alternately. The streams widened out into meres or lakes and often we found ourselves going round and round. It would be some little time before we could control the boat.

There was a little island in one of these lakes, on which stood an old thatched house with an orchard. We used to pull up here to buy apples from the owner's daughter. She was always so pleased to see us and we would follow her through the orchard as she knocked the apples off the tree with a prop. We would pick them up and put them in our dress skirts, folded up to make a pocket. Those apples were just lovely and always seemed to taste better than any we had ever tasted.

The scenery was beautiful as we paddled along in our boat, passing old windmills out of order and in ruins, with others working merrily along in the breeze. The French people working in the fields would rest awhile whilst we passed and call out a merry "Bonjour, Les Anglais," which we returned heartily. It was surprising the way they worked from morn till eve and we often saw Sisters of Mercy working alongside them. Every vegetable was cleansed and washed in the canals, laid out in the sun to dry and then packed into the punts waiting to be taken to market. It was always a pleasure to buy vegetables in France; they were all so wonderfully kept and clean. In England, we leave all the dirt on them, just as they are dug up and they are sold that way.

We used to pull our punt up under the same old tree with a hayrick at the side in order to prepare our lunch. Two sisters would set out the lunch, whilst the others would go off to explore the countryside and visit the churches, of which there were many in each village. Once I was left alone in the boat whilst the others gathered forget-me-nots, which grew in great quantities around the area. Everything was so peaceful, with just the sweet twitterings of the birds, an occasional bleating of a sheep or the moo of a cow. I soon began to get sleepy – having been up all night, the open air tended to make me so – when 'crack! crack! bang! bang!' Our anti-aircraft were busily at work. They had sighted Jerry trying to take photographs.

I saw the girls in the distance put their backs to a hayrick and prepare to stay until the firing ceased. If only I could get to that rick, but I dare not move as shrapnel was falling everywhere, and I knew that the tree under which we were anchored would protect me better than anything else from those flying pieces. The attack was soon over and the girls ran to the boat, scrambled in and we were soon on our way home none the worse for our trip. The remainder of my night duty passed almost calmly. We often got scares from Jerry but no actual bombing in our vicinity.

I was taken off night duty in December and put into the theatre, assisting with operations. I loved this work and was always thankful to be so fortunate in being assigned to the theatre. Christmas began to draw near and arrangements were made to give the boys as good a time as possible. A piano was obtained and taken to the convalescent ward. A number of us sisters scoured the countryside for holly and evergreens, but there was very little to be found.

However, we met a French officer who was an interpreter to the British Army. He was billeted at a French house and came out to see if he could help. When we explained our difficulty he said for us to come along with him. He took us into the garden of some French baron who was away and got the gardener to give us as much holly as we could carry. We thanked him profusely, our hearts gladdened because our boys would see a little of the old home Christmas in a strange land. How they cheered when they saw us enter the wards laden with the bright berried branches.

Christmas Eve came and we gathered together in the courtyard of the hospital to sing carols. Everyone who had a flash-light or candle-lantern was invited to bring it along; also their hymnals. Padre even appeared with a small harmonium and the *personelle*. We went up the steps into the hallway and sang at the top our voices, 'Whilst Shepherds Watched'. The ward doors were immediately thrown open and we all walked around the wards in twos, threes and fours, singing all the time. Not a whisper came from the patients; they were as quiet as mice. We went into each ward this way, then over to the isolation block.

I have often seen pictures of carol singers, candles in hand and faces raised, singing with all their hearts; but I am quite sure if an artist could have been there that night, a picture would have found its way into the academy that would have made the artist famous. The sisters with their white head-dress, hymn book and candle or flash-light in hand; the boys in khaki, leaning over their shoulders; the Padre with the harmonium and the patients, hardly discernible in the flickering candle light in their blanket-covered beds. I often looked back and thought what a beautiful picture it would have made.

It was midnight before we got to our beds. We had had a very busy day, preparing for the morrow. Stockings had to be filled for each boy. These were filled from the material sent by the Red Cross: socks, mufflers, caps, gloves, handkerchiefs, pips, cigarettes, tobacco and matches, pencils, writing pads, candles, etc.

Christmas dawned and with it snow. It was a beautiful white world that met our eyes. We arose and went downstairs for breakfast and were met by Santa Claus at the door of the dining room. He had a big basketful of small parcels which he beckoned us to take. We each took one. I am ashamed to say our surprise had been so great we forgot to thank him and wish him a Happy Christmas. It was our Assistant Matron, who had bought a wig and mask, who had dressed herself up in a red screen cover, trimmed with white wool! She made a beautiful Father Christmas, as she had such a commanding figure. We heard from our patients that she had been around the wards quite early with her basket, wishing them all a Happy Yuletide.

Early Service had also been held, and any patients who wished, had taken Communion. It was a great day for the boys and they had a very nice dinner of roast beef, brussels sprouts, potatoes, Christmas pudding, jellies, blancmange, coffee, cigarettes and candies.

In the evening a concert was given by the 'Harlequins'. The *personelle* had been practising for this for weeks. All the patients who possibly could get down were allowed to see the performance. It was very good and everyone thoroughly enjoyed it.

Boxing Day, the sisters and VADs gave a concert. We called ourselves the 'Fireflies' and had been practising for quite a long time. A sketch was given which lasted half an hour, and we had several songs with actions. I gave a Dutch dance, dressed in a Dutch boy's suit and clogs (sabots). The concert ended by the singing in costume of all the Allied national anthems. It was a huge success; so much so, that we had to give it over again to the Headquarters Staff and different officer friends; also French civilians. This time it was given in the afternoon and we had tea afterwards.

Things went on much as usual after Christmas and New Year. The wards were very busy, as we had received a lot of gassed patients. Poor lads, they were so ill. They could not see out of their eyes, many were very badly burned and their breathing was terrible. The sisters in these wards were kept on their toes, continually attending the patients' eyes and giving them oxygen. We also had about twenty Australian sisters who had come down from CCS which had been badly bombed; they told us that three of their sisters had been killed, along with quite a number of patients.

One of these sisters we used to call 'Fat Australian Kate'! She was a motherly old soul, whom I will never forget. She was the first one to make us get under our beds during air raids, and it was the funniest sight to see Kate, with her tin hat and silk nightdress on, bobbing out from under the bed with always the same question, "Has he gone?"

Orders came through for a number each day to take instructions in gas drill. We went down, twenty in number, to the 10 Stationary Hospital, about twenty minutes' walk from our hospital. We first had a lecture, then the drill, and then the test. With our masks fixed firmly in position, we entered a small hut, seething with lachrymatory gas. All the masks were pronounced correct and we were allowed to go on. Afterwards we were all given gas masks and steel helmets.

Saturday morning in St. Omer was always market day and we loved to be off-duty in the morning and go to see the proceedings. Nothing was brought in killed and it was the funniest sight to see a man buying his Sunday dinner. One often saw a man or woman going home with a live fowl or rabbit in the bottom of a string bag, or men putting a sack and sling over their shoulders with baby pigs squealing and struggling inside. Everybody seemed to come in to sell his goods. Old men and women with faces like parchment; the women with beautiful white caps and aprons, but with shoulders very bent from constantly working in the fields. There were also a quantity of eggs, but they were so expensive – half a franc each – but even that was cheap to what they were in England.

Another ritual on Saturday mornings was to visit our Club, an institution formed by her Royal Highness, the Princess Victoria. I do not know what we sisters and VADs would have done without these clubs. We had our tea rooms, reading and writing rooms and lounges, also a bathroom for sisters coming down the line, where baths were things of the past.

Sunday Divine Services were held in the Hospital Chapel or several little churches in town. These were used as recreation rooms for the boys during the week and often concerts and movies were given. Sisters were always invited and the first two rows of seats always reserved for us and they would never allow us to pay! These little programmes were appreciated by the boys and were a very [*good?*] thing, too.

Home Leave: February 1918

About the middle of February 1918, Matron called me into her office and told me my orders were through for a CCS (Casualty Clearing Station). How pleased I was, as this had been my ambition since arriving in France. But a few days afterwards she told me our Principal Matron had given orders for several of us to go on leave and I was to be packed and ready for when my date came through. We were supposed to have leave every six months, but we all came out *en masse* and had to go home in turns, waiting for the others to come back.

On February 21st, 1918, six of us started for leave by the ten a.m. train to Boulogne. We embarked about three p.m. and were soon on our way across the Channel. It was a very stormy crossing and several of us had to retire to the saloon, suffering from sea-sickness and not seeming to care what became of us. About seven p.m. we arrived in Folkestone, caught the next train and were soon on our way to London.

Arriving in London, we hired a taxi and drove to the Berners Hotel, not caring to continue our journey until the next morning, as we were still not quite feeling well. The next day saw us all right and very excited at the thought of meeting our people so soon. We sent telegrams and then looked at the shops. At two p.m. I caught the train for Nottingham, which arrived about six. My sister was awaiting me at the station; it was good to see her again. We soon reached home and the rest of my family had so many questions for me.

Food conditions in England at this time were very bad. How some of the less fortunate people had lived was ever a marvel to me. I knew this and had come prepared, bringing a little butter, tea and sugar. When they saw these items, it seemed they were more pleased to see them than me; but my sister explained they had not been able to get a bit of butter for over a month and that margarine and fat of any kind were very scarce. She told me that one week they had had nothing but black treacle for their bread and they had gotten so tired of it they had resorted to eating dry bread. Meat, too, had been held up somewhere for quite a time; also bacon and cheese, making fish almost the only food obtainable. Imagine, FISH for breakfast, dinner and supper for almost a month!

Food tickets soon came out with the rationing amount per person printed on. I went up to the Food Controller's office and received mine. It was marvellous because as soon as those tickets were issued, the shops were full of meat and other things. Someone must have been hoarding it away somewhere.

I had a very pleasant holiday and returned to France and to my hospital on March 6th, 1918. Matron told me there were no further orders through; but after a fortnight's work in the hospital my orders were through for 62 Casualty Clearing Station, near Proven, Belgium.

Very Active Service: (Operation Michael) March – April 1918
On March 18th, 1918, I left 59 General Hospital, St. Omer. How sorry I

was to leave my Matron and chums. It was like leaving home all over again. Matron had been so good to us all and we just loved her. I travelled as far as Hazebroucke by train.[7] There were quite a number of sisters leaving St. Omer for the various hospitals around and I found four who were going to the same CCS as I and we soon became friends.

Arriving at Hazebroucke, we reported to the RTO (Railway Transport Officer). He telephoned to the ADMS office for orders and received word that ambulances would be sent as soon as possible to collect us; so we determined to explore the town. Hazebroucke was within shelling distance and it was from hospitals that were stationed here [*that*] we received our first patients. We were told that the Boche had been shelling that day and looking around the town we saw that quite one third of this large place was lying in ruins. 'Flanders Field'.

When we got back to the station the ambulances began to arrive and our luggage was soon hoisted up into them. We were on our way, passing through some glorious countryside. As we were nearing our journey's end we remarked on how flat the ground was. The driver told us that we were in Belgium and that all about that part was flat country.

We arrived at 62 CCS about six p.m. and received a very cold reception. No orders had been received by the sister in charge as to our coming and no place was prepared for us. However, they gave us tea, took our particulars and told us to amuse ourselves.

62 CCS was stationed at a place called 'Bandage-em' near Proven, Belgium. Bandagem was a name given by the British. The CCS was half huts and half marquees, with a big drive made of duckboards running between. Our quarters were right at the top of the camp, on one side, and the officers on the other. Our quarters were Nissen huts, divided into sections of four. The huts were all sandbagged about three feet high to prevent splinters from bombs.

The next day we went on duty. I was given two huts of thirty beds each, with the medical officer who was chief surgeon at the CCS in charge. The sister in charge informed me I had been sent up for team work, that is, travelling about to different CCS, operating on patients. A surgical team consisted of one surgeon, one anaesthetist, one sister, two RAMC, orderlies and the officers' batsmen. Sister told me she had given me those wards to get acquainted with the medical officer who was to be my team surgeon. We soon became acquainted and it was not long before we were to be on a team together.

I had only been at 62 for five days when my orders came through to proceed to 47 CCS, stationed at Rosieres, beyond Amiens. On the evening of March 23rd, 1918, ambulances came up to the end of our drive to collect our luggage. By 7.30 p.m. we had started on our way. It was quite dark by 8 p.m. and we kept the curtain down as the night was very chilly. The anaesthetist took one seat on the side of the car, the surgeon had a stretcher in the middle and I had the only other seat. After a while we prepared for sleep; but the road seemed very rugged and every now and again we heard the firing of big guns, indicating [*that*]we were near the firing line.

Around midnight we reached Bethune. The firing here seemed greater than before and we had to stop for a while, as the first car with the orderlies and batmen had had a puncture. Whilst the two drivers were mending the puncture, the boys got busy making a pot of tea. When taking a long journey like this, the boys were always provided with rations: tea, sugar, bread, butter, bully beef (corned beef) and pickles. They brought us a drink of tea in a shaving cup belonging to my surgeon. What cared we? – that tea was nectar!

We had not gone far when our car had a puncture, so we had another rest. Then again we were held up at Doullens by an air raid, but not for too long. About eight a.m. we arrived at Amiens, [*and*] we were all exhausted. We put up at an hotel near the main street, not far from the station, and there we rested until breakfast was prepared for us. After breakfast we had a look around the town, each going off on his own. I was the first to get back to the hotel and had my handcase put into the ambulance. The others soon appeared and we were ready to start. We each brought a supply of fruit, as we did not know when we should be able to get any more.

We continued our journey about ten o'clock. The country was looking beautiful as we raced along. Several times we lost our way, but were put right by drivers of passing lorries. About one p.m. we arrived at Rosieres. What a place it was too! There was not a house or building that had not been peppered with bullets, some lying in absolute ruin. The people looked tired and care-worn and some had a look of anxiety on their faces. They rushed out of their houses when they saw our cars arriving and we heard their cries: "Les Anglais, Les Anglais!"

About half a mile from the village was stationed 47 CCS, on a big piece of open ground, and at the side of 47 CCS was 55 CCS. Never will I forget the sight that met our eyes. There was a constant stream of patients coming in with nowhere to put them. Marquees were being put up everywhere and stretchers taken in with the patients lying on them, their bandages blood-stained. Hundreds of milder cases were lying about in the open, getting what attention they could. Everybody was rushing about and the place was in absolute chaos.

It seemed to me that I was right on the battlefield. It was terrible to see those poor boys limping about, helping themselves as best they could. Some had fractures and their wounds were all oozing. The sisters were busy in the wards with the more serious cases and the orderlies were rushing here and there, trying to erect shelter for the night or carrying food to the patients. There was a constant stream of patients being taken to the theatre for operation by the stretcher bearers; and another stream of patients that had been operated on, leaving by a side door for the wards.

We looked around and could see no one who could tell us where to go – they were all so busy. Eventually the Colonel in charge came upon the scene; he asked us what work we had come for and we told him "Teamwork."

He said: "Well, I don't know why they have sent you. We have several staffs of different CCS now who have retreated down the line. However, we will do our best to accommodate you."

I was sent over to the sisters' mess, a square marquee, and my surgeon went along with the Colonel to the officers' mess. In a little while Matron came in, took my particulars and informed me that I would be for night duty, and that dinner would be in soon. After dinner, two other teams arrived. They, too, were for night duty, so we decided to try to sleep a little. We looked around the entire sisters' quarters, but everywhere was full, so we decided to try to sleep out in the open. We were awfully tired, having travelled through the night, but fortunately for us, and those poor wounded boys, the weather was glorious.

We found a table top, a piece of oilcloth and duckboard, spread our blankets over these and were soon wrapped in those blankets; but there was too much noise going on everywhere to sleep. (A duckboard was made of two pieces of wood, with strips of wood nailed across resembling a ladder, only [*with*] the bars much nearer together, preventing the feet from slipping through.) These were covered with a wire mesh-work and used as walks in the muddy and much used parts.

About four p.m. one of the other sisters, seeing us awake, brought us a cup of tea. Then we decided to get up and go down to the hospital to see what we could do for the boys. We met Matron on the way and she told us that we would not be needed for night duty after all, as there were sufficient teams working on nights.

Our camp was situated on an open piece of ground, facing the road which curved around in a semi-circle. On this road was a constant stream of traffic: lorries, ambulances, cars, guns; soldiers in column marching to and from the front line; civilians on the retreat; and wounded soldiers limping down from the field ambulance – there not being sufficient ambulances to carry them, but what cared they, so long as they got away from that Hades?

The civilians looked terribly care-worn and fatigued as they hurried along; some looked too ill to go much further. They were taking what they could of their homes, some being fortunate to have horses and carts. These were packed with children and old people, and whatever in the household line they could put in. Oxen were also hitched to carts and made to do their share in getting their owners to safety; but Oh, at what a pace they shambled along!

Mothers with babes in arms were trudging wearily along, hopelessly tired and hungry, but ever with thought of pushing on to a place of safety, care and mother love showing in their faces. We knew what that incessant traffic meant, although we schooled our hearts and tried to think that everything was well.

We went about the camp, helping where we could, trying to find shelter, changing dressings and getting food for the patients. Between nine and ten p.m. we had supper: bully beef (corned beef), pickles and a cup of tea. After that we prepared for bed. Shelter had been found for us in some of the night sisters' quarters. We were advised to unpack nothing and to sleep in our clothes, so as to be prepared, on the moment, for retreat. Mattresses had been thrown on the floor with one blanket each. These we crawled into; weary, but hoping that things would be brighter on the morrow. The traffic on the road almost soothed us to sleep. It seemed to me that I was lying on the warm seashore, listening to the mighty ocean. One almost imagined the breakers surging in until they met the rocks, sending the spray high into the air. It was one big roar.

We had not been in the blankets long before we heard the shrill 'one – two – three' of the night sergeant's whistle ordering all lights out – enemy aeroplane. Soon we heard the machines with their terrifying drone and whirr of machinery; nor did they seem very far away. On they came,

A new ward at the County Hospital Lincoln, where Beatrice worked before the war.

Group of nurses, with Beatrice to the left.

Beatrice in outdoor uniform.

Another group photo, with Beatrice second from the right.

Group photo, with Beatrice front centre.

Outdoor uniform.

Charles Hopkinson, Beatrice's younger brother, who was killed during the War.

Family group showing (from the left) Charles, Beatrice, Gertrude and Wilfred.

Portrait of Beatrice when she was at the County Hospital, 1916.

Damaris Hopkinson (Beatrice's mother), with Beatrice's sister Gertrude on her knee.

George Hopkinson – Beatrice's father.

D I A G R A M.

The shell had been fired from the battery
in the direction pointed by the arrow, passing so it
seemed, over the three huts and burying itself in the
ground between the huts and a bell tent, missing a Sister
in her bed by about twelve inches. We figured the shell
must have come in this direction:-

If it had passed through the windows of
the hut, as claimed by the Sisters, we figured it would
have comes so:-

You may guess these Sisters came in for
a good deal of bantering afterwards, but they took it in
good part.

Sketched diagram from Beatrice's
memoir, showing the moving
missile.

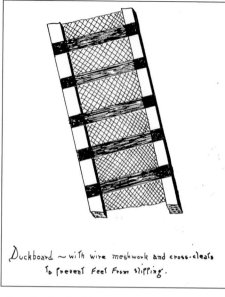

Duckboard ~ with wire meshwork and cross-cleats
To prevent feet from slipping.

Sketch of a duckboard from Beatrice's
memoir.

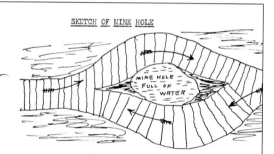

SKETCH OF MINE HOLE

MINE HOLE
FULL OF
WATER

Sketched diagram from
Beatrice's memoir, showing
the mine hole.

We found this road very tiring and
difficult to travel over, and had to hang on to the car
to keep from being thrown out.

It was on this road that we saw some
Australians with one of the big "Bouncing Bertha" guns
which they had captured from the Germans, being pulled
by a German lorry. That must have been a very rough
journey for those "Aussies" as the German lorry had no
rubber tires. They had just plain iron wheels, as the
Germans had no rubber those days.

We passed through miles and miles of barbed
wire of the Hindenberg line, and were soon at Bellicourt-
a city of white dust, from constant bombardment of the
Allies and the Germans. Here we left the ambulance,
which proceeded on its way to Ectrees for the mail. It
was to stop at Bellicourt on its way back and pick us up.

Descending a hill which was almost hidden
by the road, we came to the canal side. This canal was
absolutely hidden by the high hills on either side.
Huts and dugouts of every description were everywhere
on the hillside, giving the appearance of a town on the
hill by the river. Small wooden bridges spanned the
canal at intervals. It was on one of these small
bridges that two of our boys - a private and a corporal,
won the "Victoria Cross" for bravery, holding the
Germans back and preventing them crossing the bridge.

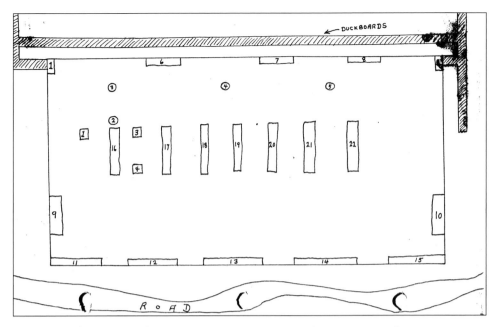

Diagram of the wards at the Casualty Clearing Stations – from Beatrice's diary.

Sketch of the Church of Saint Bertain.

Beatrice and her three sons.

Charles and Beatrice
Aylen.

Charles in later life.

Beatrice in later life.

Charles Aylen, and inset, in his army uniform.

Beatrice sewing, possibly repairing her uniform.

Group of nurses.

dropping bombs as they came. It felt [*as though*] they were as near as they possibly could be to our hut roof without damaging themselves. They could see the constant line of retreat and were not going to let anyone get away with a whole skin if they could help it. The dead and wounded from the bombing were being picked up and brought into our CCS, swelling the ranks of an already too congested camp.

It was very little sleep we got that night, as they came in relays until dawn, but we were only too thankful to be alive after the horrors of the night to care very much. Sunday morning dawned clear and beautiful, with a glorious sunrise. It seemed that we must have dreamt the happenings of the night, for it was so peaceful where we lay, except for the continuous roar which by this time we had almost gotten used to.

We arose, had breakfast and went on duty. The night sisters were still very busy at their operating tables, so I decided to get my table in order. A surgical team always carried its own operating table and outfit; with the exception of bowls, gloves, sutures and lotions. These were found by the CCS we visited. My orderlies already had the Primus stoves working. These helped to swell the noise of the retreating parties on the road. I can tell you when there are about twenty Primus stoves working together in one room, there is some noise!

The theatre was a big Nissen hut. I will try to draw a diagram so as to give some idea of what it was like. Large acetylene lamps were suspended from the ceiling. Natural light in the daytime was also received from the centre of the ceiling, from big windows running the length of the theatre. These were covered at dusk, not allowing a particle of light to escape to Jerry's quick eye.

We were soon in the midst of operating; one case being brought in as the other was ready to go out. The stretcher was placed on the table with the patient on. This saved a lot of lifting and needless pain to the patient. The anaesthetist started with the anaesthetic and by the time the sister and surgeon had scrubbed up, the patient would be almost under. White rubber gowns, called *jaconettes* were used by all. These were washed by the orderlies when we went to meals, which were very irregular during a 'push'. White cotton sterilized gowns were only used for special cases, such as skull and abdominal, as washing was so very hard to get done and dried. Two soldiers were kept busy all the time washing out towels and gowns, which were often used wet, sterilized in a push. Another two were kept busy sterilizing dressings and gloves.

The sister in charge of the theatre was kept busy all day cutting up dressings and filling drums for sterilizing; so the 'machine' went on – each one too busy to mind what the other was doing; the teams at the seven operating tables working their hardest.

The day passed along very quickly and it was soon time for the night people to arrive. We had a very awkward time at our table, as soon as it got dusk; there were only six lights over the first six tables, and we had to finish our operating by the aid of candles and torch-light. We counted up our operations, and the list was twelve; some of them had been very big operations too. We seemed to have run into a lot of amputations. My surgeon earned the name of 'Count Lop-it-off', much to our amusement and that of the other teams. It was such raillery that helped pass over the gruesomeness of our surroundings.

There was a lull in the theatre during the change from day to night staff. It was then [we] realized how tired we were; so after cleaning up our respective parts, and leaving the tables quite ready for the night staff, we departed for supper (again bully beef, camouflaged!) and bed. We retired as early as possible after our evening ablutions (a wash down in about a pint of water, and lucky to get that) and hoped to get some sleep before the arrival of Jerry, for we knew he would arrive as soon as the moon was up to any decent height. The retreat was still continuing and had been all day; it was an inevitability that he would be there to stop the incessant stream. We wondered how soon we would be joining it.

About nine p.m. mingling with the other noises was heard a bugle call, which came from the direction of 55 CCS. We arose and went out to see what it was and learned it was calling in the personnel, who were sleeping under anything they could find to shelter them from the night's chilliness; in some cases only a blanket to cover them. We also learned they had received orders to retreat. Things looked very black to us, but we were hopeful as we lay down on our mattresses again, the thought cheering us that our CCS had not as yet received orders to retreat.

Jerry soon arrived and continued as the night before. I often wondered where our planes were, also guns, as there seemed to be no opposition. Jerry had the field to himself and the laurels, if any, were his. At dawn, as before, he departed leaving a large number of dead and mangled forms behind him. We got up that morning feeling another night of horror past, and we still spared; but for how long? He had missed the CCS so far, but would he continue to do so?

On duty we went. Work must go on amongst it all. There did not seem a vacant spot in the camp. The marquees were full to overflowing; patients lying all around, with their bandages all blood-stained. The retreating on the road had never ceased and the poor boys came limping in; one boy with a fractured arm and smashed head, helping another with a fractured leg, etc., and often one saw our boys, though very badly wounded themselves, helping a more badly wounded German soldier. Perhaps, who knows, the one who had given him his wound.

We toiled through the operations that day – sixteen in all at our table, and in the evening our last case died on the table. He had been hit in the jaw with a bullet and was bleeding to death; the bullet having pierced the oesophagus and a major blood vessel. Tracheotomy was his only salvation, which we proceeded to do with the aid of an electric torch. We had just finished the operation when he passed away. Never will I forget the gruesomeness of that operation. Thoroughly upset, we cleared away and made ready for the night, but we could not forget.

We had just finished supper when the 'all lights out' warning came. We huddled like lost sheep together in our mess, not caring to go to our mattresses and [*spent*] another sleepless night, for it helped a great deal having someone to talk to. [*The*] Colonel came in and told us if we heard guns being fired not to be afraid. He said one of our big naval guns had been placed just over the road, almost over the spot I had seen a digging party early in the day, very busy at work. I called my surgeon's attention to it, thinking they were making trenches, but he informed me they were digging graves to bury the dead. He said our death roll was colossal. The 'boom, boom' of that gun as it sent out its deadly message gave us fresh courage, for we felt something was being done at last.

It was about ten p.m. on March 23rd, 1918[8] when our Colonel came and told us to get our hats and coats on with all speed, and to await his orders. He soon returned and hurried us down to several waiting ambulances. As much luggage as could possibly be gotten in for us to sit on top [*of*] had been packed in.

How we hated to leave those boys, even though we risked our lives. They were so helpless and not able to run, but how brave they were, and how pleased, to use their own words, that the womenfolk were going away from it all. [At this point in the manuscript Beatrice includes four lines from 'The Vigil' by T.A. Girling.]

Into the ambulances we got and the driver started slowly on his way, keeping under the shadow of the trees. Fortunately, Jerry had ceased his little play for a while. I think it was for this lull our Colonel had waited. On to Amiens we went – at last joining that moving stream. We arrived in Amiens about one-thirty a.m. and reported at the 42 Stationary Hospital there.

The Sister told us they did not know what to do with us, but we could join the crowd, showing us a small oblong room. We soon knew what she meant by 'crowd'. Lying on the floor, packed closely together like sardines, were about fifteen sisters who had earlier in the evening retreated from their CCS.[9] One or two awoke and looked lazily at us, too tired to care who the newcomers might be.

We decided the only thing to do was to lie down and help fill that 'sardine tin'. [*We had*] nothing but a piece of cold oilcloth and the clothes we had on as a cover, and the night was very cold with a tinge of frost. One of our sisters came up and told us the cook in the kitchen had made a big bucket of tea and that it was in the Padre's room. Poor Padre had given up his room and bed to the sisters; where he was, I do not know.

(The next morning the Padre's batman went to call him as usual and was so nonplussed at the sight of the sisters on the floor, plus three in the Padre's bed, that he did not know what to do! Stepping over the sisters on the floor, he took hold of one of them in the bed and asked "Excuse me, is the Padre here?" Padre often told this yarn afterwards. I suppose he was greatly amused.)

On arriving in the Padre's room we found a big steaming bucket of tea and a few enamel basins. We dipped in the bucket with the basin and drank greedily. There were also some dry biscuits which we enjoyed; afterwards returning to our sardine box and soon to sleep. I often awoke during the night, hearing Jerry over the town, but I was too tired to care. It was the cold I was minding the most.

Morning came all too soon, and we arose with very stiff limbs; we were told to go over to the sisters' mess, situated in another part of the town, for breakfast. On our way through the town, we noticed what a lot of devastated buildings there were. We were then told it was from the bombing of the night before and somehow we had slept through almost all of it. I have often heard our boys say, "Oh, you get used to it Sister", when I have asked them how could they sleep with the guns roaring, and now we were doing exactly that. The sisters on duty at 42 Stationary

Hospital that evening told us they had had 47 deaths that night in the hospital.

Breakfast over, we walked aimlessly about the town, wondering if Jerry had captured our CCS or not; when whom should we meet but two of our surgeons from 47 CCS. They were very dusty and tired, having tramped so far. At intervals they had been picked up by lorries and had that way managed to reach Amiens. We asked them; "But what of the CCS?" and they told us that almost all the patients had been taken safely away by ambulances and lorries; only twenty remained and these were carried in relays by orderlies to the nearest dressing station. Afterwards the CCS was burned down so that the Boche could not get anything. That was very cheering news, for we had worried for those that remained. We heard also that 36,000 patients had passed through the CCS in those few days.

Amiens at this time was in a terrible state. Civilians and troops were marching in all the time; everything was so disorganised. The military police and traffic police [were] nobly trying to keep order, but it was impossible – the invasion had been so swift and great. To get food in any of the cafés was almost impossible. We finally did manage to secure a little refreshment at the station buffet; afterwards reporting again at 42 Stationary, where we were told to be in readiness to proceed to Abbeville, to the nurses' home.

We were feeling pretty hopeless by this time, news having been received that the Germans were advancing rapidly and that our troops were just fleeing before their onslaught. What would be the end of it all? Would we in the end have to submit to German rule, defeated?

About two p.m. we boarded ambulances, sitting on the box seat with the drivers as the cars were full of patients from 42 Stationary: they, too, were going to join that endless stream. We had not gotten started when we received orders that we were not the sisters to go; so, down we got and awaited our turn. About three p.m. the hospital was empty – beds left just as the patients had been taken out, and everything strewn about. Absolute chaos reigned everywhere.

We, who were left from 47 CCS started in mechanical fashion to tidy up, not having much heart for anything. But we did not wait long before we were in the thick of it again. Patients were pouring in from everywhere and, much to my pleasure, two of my patients we had operated on the previous day at 47. I recognized the little officer fellow by his gold charm, a little thumbs-up on his neck, supposed to be for luck. Possibly some fond mother or sweetheart had put it on his neck before his leaving for the front, hoping in some way to keep him safe. I don't think he ever saw the War again, as we had excised his left elbow joint. He told us what we already knew of the CCS. Food was soon provided; dressings re-arranged and, in several cases, operations done.

In a little while more sisters came and took over the hospital and we were told to go and get our supper. This we tried to do but most of the cafés would not serve us. They all seemed to be packing and making ready for flight. In some cases we were informed, "*Anglais No Bonne* [sic] – let Germans through!" We thought we might get food at the station where we had taken lunch, earlier in the day, but they too were in a state of chaos.

It was coming away from the station that we noticed a YMCA hut with its welcome red triangle over the door, so we decided to go there and get what food we could. We got a very nice supper of bread and butter, hard boiled eggs and coffee, served on cardboard box lids. Officers round about gave us chocolates and we thoroughly enjoyed our meal.

On our return to the hospital we were told to go to the officers' hospital[10] at the other end of the town for the night; and in the morning we should receive fresh orders. About twenty of us proceeded on our way, handcases in hand, and had just gotten on the boulevard when we heard Jerry above. There had been no warning. Jerry had given that himself by dropping a few bombs.

In a few seconds we were in the midst of it; machine gun fire, anti-aircraft and bombs. There was no place to shelter, only under the tall trees, and we were just half-way between the two hospitals, so we decided to proceed with all possible haste. How I wished for my steel helmet. We put our small handcases on our heads, hoping if any bullets or shrapnel should fall on us they would lessen the blow. How they came, striking the cobbles and making sparks fly. In the midst of it all we heard a cry and looked around to find two of our sisters and MO (Medical Officer) had been hit with a piece of shrapnel in the leg. Evidently the wounds were not severe, as they were able to limp back to the 42nd Hospital, where they were operated on right away and sent down the line. I might mention that these sisters received the Military Medal afterwards.[11]

Terrified, we ran and soon reached the hospital. What a relief to get under its roof. Anything was better than being out in the open, even though it might come crumbling down on top of us in a few minutes. Jerry was certainly out to do mischief that night. How we escaped is a marvel to me. In the darkness we found our way about as best we could. We were informed by some RAMC boys left in charge, that all the sisters had left earlier in the day and the patients had been sent to a place of safety.

I seemed to get separated from the rest of the sisters and, in the darkness, got lost. The place was very bewildering. I heard automobiles drawing up in front of the hospital and there seemed to be a great commotion everywhere. Jerry was still very busy and our guns were making a terrible noise trying to get him down. I tried to find the front doors, where I heard the cars still arriving and voices. As I got nearer I heard moans and realized that they were again filling the hospital with wounded. Stumbling along, I found myself in a ward. Beds seemed to be placed in every direction and in the darkness I could hear the moaning and breathing of patients. Every available spot on the floor was filled with stretchers with patients on them, where they had been placed hastily to get them under cover from the inferno outside.

For an hour I worked, getting drinks of water and making the boys as comfortable as I possibly could in the darkness. I had found three patients dead on their stretchers and others seemed almost pulse-less. I got one of the boys to bring in the MO, who was busy in another part and asked him for brandy for the patients whom I thought it might revive. He brought a bottle and, not having a corkscrew, we knocked the neck of the bottle off on the wall.

Never will I forget that night; working in the darkness, stumbling over stretchers, getting drinks and tending the boys. I cannot describe it. Even now, when I think of finding those boys dead on their stretchers a shudder goes through me. It was gruesome.

For a few minutes Jerry ceased his play of dropping bombs and gunfire. This enabled me to have a small light and I decided to try to find my way back to the other part of the hospital, where I had left the other sisters. I soon heard their voices and this guided me to where they were. In a small square room, seated round an oval table, they sat. They had found provisions and having made tea, were eating their supper. It looked so peaceful that for a moment I thought I was dreaming. I stood, it seemed, for a few moments by the door without speaking. They all stopped talking and turned towards me asking, "Whatever is the matter?" I must have looked a bit wild – my dress and hands blood-stained, still clutching the hurricane lamp. "For God's sake!" I cried, sitting on a chair and fighting a great desire to weep. "Come and help me!"

After I had explained, they all made ready and came along with me to help the patients. They had heard nothing of the arrival of the ambulances and knew nothing about the scene I had witnessed. On arriving back to the patients, we first fastened up all the windows and doors, so no light could shine outside for Jerry's eager eyes to see. Then started the work of getting as many of the boys as we possibly could into bed, and giving them something to eat and drink. Some of the boys needed immediate operations; others anaesthetic to set a limb. There were some very nasty fractures. No wonder those poor boys cried out when I had stumbled over them earlier in the darkness.

By two a.m. we had the boys feeling fairly comfortable and, as relief had come for us from 42 Stationary Hospital, we were allowed to go to our beds to try to get a little sleep. But sleep was impossible owing to the fiendish noise created by Jerry and our anti-aircraft guns. I was quite sure we would not escape a bomb that night, as they seemed to be getting nearer and nearer all the time. One did fall in a garden next to the hospital, catching a building as it came on its downward way of destruction and sending debris clattering into the hospital yard. We could not rest in our beds whilst Jerry was so active and again found our way downstairs, wishing we had been allowed to stay on duty with the boys.

Somehow we did not seem to mind the air raids if we were busy tending to our patients' needs. They, poor things, were always more restless and needed more attention during an air raid and we had to be brave for their sakes. Sometimes it was a great effort. I have often given words of comfort to the boys with a very steady voice, but with my knees simply knocking together, but they did not know it.

It was getting light, and about four a.m. when Jerry finally gave up his play. We crawled into bed, fully dressed and slept soundly until seven. Arriving downstairs about seven-thirty we found breakfast of bread and butter, boiled eggs and tea.

I had hardly gotten through my breakfast when I heard my surgeon's [*team surgeon*] voice outside the door. He came in looking very pale and haggard, at which I remarked, and he told me that whilst dining the night before, he had almost been killed by a bomb. They were sitting at dinner in the hotel close to the station, when a bomb crashed through the hotel to the room where they were, killing an officer at their table who had refused to get under it. Undoubtedly, the surgeon too would have been killed, as there were pieces of bomb everywhere and most of their dinner plates had been smashed, with cutlery bent into almost unrecognizable shapes.

My surgeon had arrived to take me down to Boulogne. He had received orders for us to proceed to 55 General Hospital, Wimereux, Boulogne, where we were to report for duty. We drove to Amiens Station, to see if by any chance our luggage had arrived there. Imagine my surprise and pleasure when I found mine. I thought it would have been lost forever. This was put into our ambulance and away we went. I was very thankful, as the Boche had already started putting shells into Amiens and our troops were just fleeing before him. Everything was disorganized for the time being. I shall never forget how utterly hopeless I felt on that journey and I could see that my surgeon and anaesthetist felt the same, although they said very little about it.

About three p.m. we arrived at a little village and, noticing a YMCA hut, my surgeon suggested we go to see if we could get something to eat as we had had nothing since breakfast. The officer in charge of the YMCA received us very kindly, made us fresh tea, gave us cakes and chocolates and water with which to wash. He really seemed to go out of his way to be kind to us and was very eager to receive news when we told him where we had come from. When we left he had us put our autographs in his book.

Interlude: Boulogne, late March – 11 April 1918
We arrived in Boulogne about seven p.m., very dusty and tired, with our heads aching frightfully. We soon reached 55 General Hospital and I was sent into supper, which was just at that moment being served. All eyes seemed to be turned my way and before I had been at the table very long I was besieged with questions. They knew things were not as they [were] thought to be 'up the line' and being 'down at the base' they did not get the news very quickly.

I had no appetite for supper, but the cup of tea I found very refreshing to my parched and dusty throat. How peaceful everything seemed here. I could hardly realize in such peaceful surroundings that I had been through, what seemed a horrible nightmare.

I received word that Matron was waiting to see me, so I hastened to her room. "My child," she said, "I know what you must have gone through and I don't want to hear a word about it. Just go to bed and rest and stay there all day tomorrow." I tried to protest, but Matron was very firm. When I arrived at my bedroom, the sisters who had sat at my table had gotten my keys, put up my bed, got out my bath and made a roaring fire in the grate. All I had to do was to undress, jump into the bath and then into bed. How kind everyone was, I thought, and then I burst into tears for which I felt much better, thereafter falling asleep soundly until I heard a knock at my door, and there appeared a VAD with a breakfast tray.

I felt very refreshed after my sleep – the first real sleep I had had for a week; also the first time for a week I had been undressed. Needless to say, I ate everything on that tray and after washing, fell into a sound sleep until dinnertime.

That night about midnight Jerry came. I got up and went into the next hut, to the sister there, trembling from head to foot and my teeth chattering in my head. But it was soon over and I was able to go back to bed. The next morning I was put on duty in a hut of thirty patients. Casualties were arriving hourly, straight from the firing line. Some of the poor boys had bled so much we had to soak them off their stretchers. Most of the sisters had never been 'up the line' and were horrified at the condition of the patients; I told them that was nothing to what we had sometimes had to witness.

For a fortnight we worked hard. Wounded were just pouring in and the patients who were able to travel were sent to Blighty. Then our team received orders to report again to 62 CCS at Bandeghem, where we had started out from. Being a team, we knew what that meant – somewhere another offensive where we were to go and help out again.

It was with mixed feelings that I left 55 General Hospital on the morning of April 11th, 1918. Everyone had been so kind and there had been no air raids, with the exception of the short one on the second night of my arrival. Then there was the sea; I had missed that and hated to leave. Hours I had sat on the sands and listened to its mighty boom. Sometimes at night I had followed the tide out for miles. It was all so lovely.

About ten a.m. our ambulances arrived and after many goodbyes and god-speeds we started off on our travels again. It was a beautiful morning and everything was looking so fresh and nice. About midday we arrived in St. Omer, and parked our cars in the Place Victor Hugo, before going for lunch. The officers went to the officers' club, which was very near. I decided to go to 58 General Hospital to see my old matron and friends I had left behind when I went to 62 CCS.[12]

Matron was in her office and was so surprised and pleased to see me. She sent me down to the sisters' mess, where I got some lunch and saw my chum who was on night duty. Other friends were on duty in the hospital, where they were so busy; simply crowded out with patients, who were lying in every available spot. I only visited a few minutes, and then said good-bye.[13] My surgeon was waiting for me, so away we started again, arriving at 62 CCS about 5 p.m. just in time for tea.

Bandaghem to St Omer, via Watten: Operation Georgette, mid-April – mid-May 1918

There were joyous cries from the sisters when they saw us return, and how they hugged me, saying, "Why we were sure you had been killed; we heard such awful stories." The Sister-in-charge of the CCS came in and took me very kindly by the hand. My surgeon turned to her and said, "I have brought her back Matron; and she does you credit." I never quite knew what he meant and Matron never informed me.

In the morning I went to the theatre, but there was very little to do in the operating line, excepting preparation: cutting dressings for sterilizing, packing gloves, cleaning instruments and sterilizing sutures etc.

Three days after my arrival we were warned to be prepared for casualties and had barely received the warning when wounded commenced to pour rapidly in.[14] Operations began immediately. It appeared, so we were told, that our offensive and the manner in which it was to be carried out had been planned, and the day before our troops had gone over the top. The Boche came over the top and did exactly what our army had planned to do. I believe this was at Passchendaele.

A great many of the wounded [*in*] those days were French and we were kept busy for about a month; going on duty at seven-thirty a.m. and working sometimes until four a.m. the next morning, with just two hours off in which to rest. Meals were very irregular these days for the teams in the theatre. We often thought we had just time to do another small operation before lunch, and what would appear to be a small one would turn out to be most complicated, taking a few hours. Sometimes it would be after three p.m. before we would get lunch. It was just the same with dinner at night, which we occasionally would not get until after nine p.m. Then we often had to go back and clear up, making no extra work for the night staff.

Very often, if there was a colossal waiting list of operations and the wounded kept pouring in, we would only rest until midnight, and then go on duty again until four a.m., with one other day sister coming to relieve us. That meant six a.m. before one got to bed, as there was so much clearing [*up*] to do. Getting up at eight a.m. we would then start the same routine. This only happened during an offensive and one willingly gave [*one's*] all to those poor boys.

Jerry too, was very busy as usual. When an offensive was on, we always knew what to expect. Night after night he came along with his machine gun fire and bombs; and at that time using what the boys called the 'stick bomb', which in a way was more dangerous than the other kind. The bombs used formerly made huge holes in the ground and one felt safe, if lying flat, from pieces of flying shrapnel, unless of course, it was dropped in one's immediate vicinity, whereas the stick bomb would just touch the ground and explode, killing everyone lying on the ground. They knew we always put ourselves flat on the ground during an air raid, so thought they would make something that would cure us of that habit.

Several mornings during that busy month we found bullets which had pierced our Nissen huts, mess, cook house etc., but no damage was done and no one wounded, which was extremely fortunate. Every day, too, we went about in fear of a shell being put into our camp, as the Boche were shelling very badly. If was funny to hear the boys – those out on rest – when asked how they got wounded: "Oh, I was just passing by 'Hellfire Corner' Sir, when Jerry put a shell over," or "I was working by 'Salvation Corner'," and such like appropriate names which had been given on some remembered day that well earned its name.

After a month's busy time, we got orders for the CCS to move, as we were in direct line of shell fire, and we were all sent to 10 CCS at Arneke, where we stayed until May 14th, 1918. The first week or so were very busy and there was only one air raid. I often helped out in the wards here, as there was not sufficient operating to keep us busy.

On May 14th, 1918, sixty-two CCS staff left 10 CCS and proceeded to a place called Watten, where they had placed the CCS. Our mess and sleeping quarters were in a gorgeous orchard. How peaceful it all was, but we were not to do any work here at all as our orders came through the next morning to 'stand to' and be prepared to go to Alsace-Lorraine, where our CCS was to open up. For a week we stayed in this beautiful spot, thoroughly enjoying every minute and the rest doing us good. Long walks in the Eperleagues Forest, picnics and lorry-hopping taking up most of our time.

One night, not being able to sleep, we put on our big coats over our night attire and walked around the orchard. It was a glorious night. The moon was riding high in the heavens and we could hear the night birds cooing to one another. The stillness of the night was broken by the whirr of an enemy bomb whirling through the air and then 'bang!', swiftly followed by three others. We hastened to our marquee, grabbed our tin hats and made for the dug-out. This dug-out was a wonderful thing, made in 1914 by our boys. It was about 22 feet in length, 3 feet wide and 3 feet high; and as far as I can remember it was dug in about 4 feet. The walls and ceiling were made of pieces of tree trunks cut in half, giving it the appearance of a log cabin. The length of the dug-out on either side were seats made of stakes of wood with branches and twigs of trees interlaced, and a duckboard runner in the centre of the floor.

There were openings: one the entrance, having four steps leading down to the dug-out; the other opening leading to the trenches. Our Colonel had had the dug-out fixed up beautifully for us. The walls and seats were draped with tarpaulin sheets; a blanket hung over each opening and a hurricane lamp hung in the centre from a beam. The night policeman used to light this lamp every night in case of an air raid.

We stayed in the dug-out about an hour and, as there was no repetition of the bombs, went back to our beds and finally to sleep with our tin hats tucked under one end of the pillow. Some of the sisters, not having tin hats, put their enamel washing bowls where they could easily get them in case of Jerry returning. Many of the sisters even went to sleep with these bowls upon their chests, which often used to fall off in the middle of the night, waking us all up, when we would scramble for our different head-dress and make for the dug-out!

News from the Line these days was a little more encouraging. Our troops were holding the Boche back, but not advancing. How long it would last we did not know and daily lived in the dread of the Boche breaking through.

About the third morning of our stay in Watten we were awakened by the clanging of heavy guns and machinery, and a stampede of troops. Not knowing what to expect, we arose, hastily dressed and went out to see what all the noise was. How our hearts throbbed with happiness when we heard the "Yeps" and "Gee-whizzes" of the Yankees marching past in their thousands. How excited we were and called and cheered them. Some of the officers came up to us and asked for a drink of water, telling us they had landed at Calais and were en route, marching to different parts.

Poor boys, how tired they looked, and not used to marching. Some of them had only been in training a month before coming out to France. Ambulances were following the troops, picking up any who were feeling sick and a lorry followed too, picking up the kits which the boys were throwing in all directions. We were so happy that day for we knew that the Germans would soon be on the run. They never would be able to put up any stand against the new reinforcements.

On May 20th, 1918, the female staff had orders to proceed to 10 Stationary Hospital, St. Omer; which was also a hostel for sisters awaiting orders. We arrived at the hostel just as supper was being served. After supper, having nothing better to do, we returned to our rooms, for we had orders for duty in the morning.

I was sent to a big surgical ward holding between fifty to sixty beds, which were mostly full of heavy surgical cases from the last bombing raid, and who were soon to be bombed again. The day passed very quickly and it was soon bedtime. Feeling very tired, we retired early, but we had only been in bed what seemed a few moments when 'whirr, whirr,' we heard enemy planes overhead. Immediately the bell from the ruins of Eglise St. Bertin commenced its mournful toll and, as [*if*] by magic, every light was extinguished. We thought Jerry must have gone off in another direction as we could not hear the machines and everything was so deadly still; when 'whirr, whirr, bang, bang, bang, bang', four bombs dropped in quick succession.

Hastily snatching our blankets off our beds, we quickly wended our way in the darkness to the cellars. A rule had been made that all were to go to the cellars, where stretchers were provided. Should any sister be wounded outside of the cellars, she would be classified as self-inflicted. For an hour we stayed in that damp place, shivering and aching all over. Some of the sisters had made up their beds on the stretchers, which were hoisted on two trestles, and were sleeping, dead to everything!

About midnight we heard the doorbell clang. We put our heads through the window and saw it was the night sergeant from the hospital asking for Matron. (We could hear what he said in our room.) Soon Matron came and we overhead him say, "Matron, those four bombs fell on the Hospital, killing and wounding a great many." None of the sisters were wounded, fortunately, so all were busy doing what they could for those bombed, already-bombed, patients. There was no more sleep for us that night. We fretted because we could not help too.

In the morning my orders came through to proceed to 10 CCS, which had been moved from Arneke to Soex, near Bergues and Dunkerque. After I had my packing finished, I went with some other sisters to the hospital to see what damage had been done. Arriving at the hospital, we saw terrible destruction. The bombs had hit two top wards and cellars below, taking beds with their patients and all kinds of ward equipment with them; killing and wounding not only the patients who had not been able to get out of bed, but those patients who had gone down to the cellars for their supposed safety. We also heard that one of the MOs had been killed.

We tore ourselves away from this scene of death and destruction and, arriving at the hostel, found the ambulance awaiting us. Two other sisters were joining us for the trip to 10 CCS. It was a glorious day, bright and sunny. How we enjoyed that drive. We passed through picturesque Cassel with its many winding roads and windmills. The streets were all cobbled, and at the mount was a casino. It was rumoured that a German prince was buried here and the Germans had promised never to bomb or shell the town. As far as I know Cassel never even had a bullet hole; though the Germans often passed over in planes and it would have made a good target, owing to its high altitude.

I had a friend at the CCS in Esquelbecq and the driver took us out of our way a little so that I might call on her. Unfortunately, she had gone into St. Omer on a shopping expedition and we must have passed her on the way. We soon arrived in Wormhoudt and Soex was about four kilometres away, so it then didn't take us long to get to 10 CCS.

Late May 1918 – August 1918

10 CCS was situated in an open field under canvas, close to the main road. It was beautifully set out [*and*] had a nice avenue of trees leading right up to the sisters' mess. No patients had been received, but the sisters and personnel were kept busy getting their wards in order and erecting huts, etc., I was put in the theatre to help prepare, as I had been sent up for team duty.

For several weeks we had very little work to do, so were able to go about a great deal and see the country. We visited the quaint old town of Bergues, which had its moat, city wall and gateways – *Porte de Bergues* and *Porte de Dunkerque*. The town itself was very ancient. The streets were all cobbled and there was a beautiful cathedral which we never tired of looking around, always finding something new to admire.[15]

There was also a very high tower. I have forgotten what it was called, but I think it was 'the belfry'. An old woman was in charge of it and evidently she had been forbidden to let anyone enter; but we pressed a coin into her palm and she smuggled us in. We climbed up a narrow winding stone stairway, with steps all worn in the centre with much usage. I thought we would never get to the top; our knees were almost giving way and we were so breathless by the time we reached, what seemed to me to be, a lookout cabin of a ship.

The old lady made us understand that her father, grandfather and great-grandfather had all been caretakers before her and she showed us where they had carved their names. From this room we mounted another *special* stairway of about thirty steps and came to a room of bells; thirty-eight in all, ranging from the size of a small dinner bell to the biggest bell I have ever seen, hanging in the centre of the belfry. These bells used to chime on the hour, quarter and half hour. I heard them only once and they were very sweet.

We had not much time to look around Dunkerque, as it was some distance away and we always had plenty of shopping to do. Also, we were forbidden to stay any longer than necessary, as several times it had been bombarded from the sea, and several of the most interesting places were boarded up as they had been shelled.

One day we went down from Dunkerque to Malo les Bains and sat on the sands, watching the sea with its mysteries and secrets. Far out at sea we would see big ships, possible men-of-war [*ships*]. Malo was a pretty seaside place, but desolate and forsaken. It looked like a ghost of the past. Its many white and grey buildings empty; bathing vans and stalls helping in that picture of desolation.

Troops soon began to be billeted round about us, so we occasionally had a few mild cases. The men were out on rest. Concerts and sports were frequently given and invitations were always sent to the sisters. Often a lorry or car would be sent to take us over. Then one day, whilst most of the sisters were away at some sports, we that were left behind, received orders that about one hundred influenza cases were being sent to us. I was just up from the flu myself. Fortunately, I had not had a very bad attack, so went down to assist.

How my back and head ached before we were through. During those early days of the flu the treatment was to strip the patients in one tent, their clothing going immediately to the fumigator. Then, the patient was bathed in disinfectant and taken to the different wards. Some of the patients were very ill and died with pneumonia after a few days. We were kept very busy after this, but there was not much operating to be done, so Matron put me on night duty, in charge of 'B' and 'C' lines, which consisted of six marquees – B 1, 2 and 3 and C 1, 2 and 3. There was an orderly in charge of each marquee, which lightened the work considerably.

We had several air raids, but nothing to worry about, until one night. I was passing along the duckboard from one marquee to another, when I heard planes above and immediately machine gun fire. I did not hurry under cover at the sound of the plane, as he was so low I thought it was one of ours. I could see him distinctly, it seemed to be just above the marquee.

Whether he could see my white head dress in the moonlight, I do not know, but he appeared to be aiming for that. I hastened in C 3 lines and then I heard a scampering from C 1. Rushing through, I met some of the convalescents from C 1, "Oh Sister, Sister," they cried, "one of the men has been hit." I rushed through to C 1, and there lying on his stretcher, killed instantaneously by a bullet entering the back of his neck and penetrating through the abdominal aorta and burying itself in the floor, was one of my boys. [*An*] orderly and I picked up the stretcher and carried him into the bedded marquee, thinking there might be something we could do, but it was no use. The MO came along in his night attire, covered by a big coat, but all he could say was, "He is dead, Sister."

Jerry did not return again that night so my patients soon returned to their beds, shivering from the cold. Most of them had rushed out as they were, bare-footed and with only their night attire on. We heard afterwards that this plane was brought down at Dunkerque and both the pilot and observer were dead drunk.

Our anti-aircraft guns had kept up a very good barrage all the time Jerry was over, and several dud shells had fallen into our compound. The sisters had not had much sleep. Two Irish sisters, sharing an Armstrong hut together, were full of the raid when they came on duty that morning, and told us they had seen a dud shell go through their windows and heard it bury itself outside. We laughed at them, knowing well they could not possibly have seen a shell of that description, unless they had been immediately behind the gun it had been fired from. I think we convinced them of this afterwards. The shell certainly had fallen very close to their hut and no doubt they were terribly frightened.

It was whilst I was on night duty that I developed neuralgia in the left side of my face, which became very swollen. My surgeon became very suspicious and said, "Sister, I wonder if that is neuralgia or a blocked antrum?" Matron's permission was obtained and that day an X-ray picture taken, which showed the antrum blocked; so I was ordered down the line to the sisters' hostel at Moulle.

From Moulle, the next morning, I travelled by ambulance to Boulogne, passing through some wonderful scenery. How I hated that journey and how I hated leaving my CCS for the base. I felt I would never see my chums again. England would be my lot – so my thoughts ran. All we sisters who had been on Foreign Service hated the thought of being sent back to England on the sick list. We were so afraid of not getting back to France, even with all its horrors of war it still held a fascination for us. We felt we were doing so much more in France for our boys than in England, although we realized that someone must stay behind to tend the boys as they poured into the various hospitals in our homeland.

'Sick Sister': August 1918 – September 1918

I arrived at the Château Mauricien the morning of August 25th 1918. This was a private house loaned by an English artist to the sisters and VADs to be used in case of sickness. Everything was beautifully arranged. It truly was a haven after life under canvas. Most of the rooms were most tastefully decorated, several having fresco ceilings. One room was painted in Wedgewood blue and was very beautiful with its many mirrors and paintings. It was in this room that her Majesty, Queen Mary and her Majesty's Lady-in-waiting were entertained at dinner on their visit to France.

The next day I was sent up to the 2nd Canadian Hospital, about three miles from the Château Mauricien to see Captain Hames, a specialist on ear, nose and throat. He performed a small operation, under a local anaesthetic, [*and*] told me there had been an abscess there, but it had cleared and left a thickening of the membranes; and that was the density which showed up on the X-ray plate. I was so pleased with this news, as I had thought it might mean weeks of treatment in hospital in Blighty. He also said, "Sister, I am afraid I cannot get you to in Blighty with this." I was overjoyed with this news and exclaimed: "That is what I have been dreading – being sent home."

However, he sent me for a fortnight's rest at Hardelot, to a convalescent home in the charge of Lady Gifford. Hardelot was very near to Boulogne and on the sea front. I thoroughly enjoyed my rest there. The home was beautifully managed and the food splendid. In fact, it was just the place for an invalid. There was an officers' rest camp near, which was always full of officers. They used to arrange picnics to which the sisters were invited; also sports on the sand by the sea; hockey, basketball, cricket, etc., in which we used to take part. Then the hospital nearby was always holding concerts, so that we were thoroughly entertained and time did not hang too heavily on our hands. In fact, it went all too quickly.

The doctor saw us after a week's rest and sent those who were fit back to duty. My turn came [*on*] September 9th, 1918. We were taken by ambulance to the Hotel Du Nord, Boulogne, where we reported and received orders from the embarkation sister, whose duty it was to see our principal matron every morning.

On September 10th, 1918, I was sent back to the hostel at Moulle, there to await orders. We had a jolly time here, too; impromptu dances were arranged between ourselves. The English sisters were not allowed to dance in uniform, nor if they had an impromptu dance amongst themselves were they allowed to invite any gentlemen. This was a very strict rule in the English [*British*] Army. We thoroughly enjoyed ourselves nevertheless and each one was given three hours in which to think out a fancy dress!

Nothing was to be bought, each falling on his own resources. Seven-thirty was the time for the dance and we were to be received by our Matron in charge of the hostel in the sitting-room. She received about eight of us and then collapsed with laughter. It really was marvellous – the ingenuity of those Sisters.

One appeared as 'Boudoir', another as 'Pre-historic', another as 'Queen Anne' – my eiderdown helping to make the old fashioned ruffle around the hips – then, with the aid of sheets, we transformed a very dark Irish girl into an Indian girl, putting sandals on her feet and earthen jar upon her shoulder, each lending her little trinkets as beads, bangles, etc., to make the picture more realistic.

One costume which was very clever, and which was called 'Active Service', was made of a canvas bath mat as a skirt, canvas basin as a hat, with toothbrush as decoration, and all manner of utensils hung on a string around the waist – rubber boots completing the picture. Then there were gypsy girls, myself as cowboy and finally a nigger [*N.B. Then a commonly used term for someone of non-caucasian ethnicity*] dressed in an evening suit. This sister had us all guessing as to whom she was. We heard what an awful time she had afterwards getting off that soot.

Well I remember, too, 'Pre-historic' who was dressed in a ragged piece of canvas, arms, neck and chest bare, with autumn leaves falling in great array from her hair down her back. She wanted her skin bronzed and I suggested she use my brown shoe polish, which was liquid. We tried it, and it was just the thing, but when she came to get if off, well, I'm afraid there were many raw spots on her skin afterwards. We heard her scrubbing long after we were in bed, as she shared our room.

A whist drive was also arranged. At this we were allowed to invite any of our officer friends who might be billeted around. This, too, was a huge success.

On the Move Again: Autumn 1918, Devastated Areas

Then my orders came to report at 58 CCS, which was at Longuenesse – the other side of St. Omer. I arrived there just as supper was being served. I noticed everything was in a state of commotion, and when I asked the reason, was told that the CCS was moving on the morrow to Tincourt – a hundred miles or more further south. Matron told me after supper not to unpack much as I was for team duty, and our team, along with two others, was starting out for 62 CCS at Remy Siding (named by British) near Poperinghe; so I just fixed my bed, managing as best I could.

About 10 a.m. on the 26th September, we left Longuenesse, arriving at 62 CCS about one p.m. After dinner, our team had orders to get ready for operations, and by two p.m. we were in full swing, working hard until eight p.m. I might state that the colonel in charge was my old Colonel of 62 CCS and he was very pleased to see me. Most of the officers were also the same, but the nursing staff was all different.

The next day we were not quite so busy, so I was able to visit 10 CCS which was very close to 62, and met a great many of my old chums. They were pleased I had not been sent to England and hoped I would stay at 62 CCS so as to be near them; but the three teams that came from 58 CCS had orders to move the next morning and I was not able to even say good-bye to my chums, as we started on our way about nine-thirty the following morning. How we wished we could get to a place where we could stay for a little while. This constant packing and unpacking grew a little tiresome at times.

About nine-thirty on the morning of September 28th, 1918, a convoy of ambulances arrived, in charge of an officer with a big touring car, to take us on our journey. The luggage was soon piled into the cars and myself, along with another sister and officer, climbed into the touring car; the other sister of the party preferring to ride in the front of an ambulance.

We passed through Poperinghe, Steenvorde, Hazebrouck, Aire, Morrent, Gontes and Lillers, trying to get to St. Pol in time for lunch. A new rule had been made in France that no lunch should be served after two p.m., owing to the shortage of food. We arrived in St. Pol at just after half past two, so decided to have a lunch of the biscuits, candy and lemonade we had brought with us. So, standing on the road side, outside the town we had our lunch; then, refreshed and our cramped limbs stretched, we again boarded our cars.

It was not long before we came to Frévent and then Doullens, about four p.m., where we managed to get tea in a restaurant; boiled eggs, brown bread and butter and tea; continuing our journey about five p.m. Ten miles or so out of Doullens, the devastated areas began. It was a terrible sight for it was as though a huge comb had been at work on the buildings and the ground was all torn up with vast craters everywhere. The road we travelled along had been repaired, but in places we had to go very carefully.

We reached the, once beautiful, city of Albert about six p.m. How my heart ached for those homeless people. Albert, to me, seemed to be more devastated than any town I had seen. We stayed a little while in that dead city and looked around. Going round a bend in the road we came upon a dead German soldier. He had been missed by the clearing party and the stench from his body was terrible.

Soon we saw the Albert Cathedral lying in ruins. It had been predicted that as soon as the Madonna fell from its dome, the war would cease, and here we were after a few months travelling over the same land that we had retreated from; the Germans on the run and us gaining ground every day.

As we passed through the town of Albert, we saw a poor homeless dog, seeming to care for naught, lying on the windowsill of his old home. He looked so pathetic and very thin. We wished we could take him along with us, but we did not know what we might be taking him to, perhaps worse than what he had already gone through – who knows?

Another hour through bombed, shelled and deserted land and devastated towns, and then we came to Péronne. Here was a little life. Our troops were billeted all around in the tumble-down shacks and houses, making their billet as much a home as they could, but it was a poor attempt. We passed boys washing themselves in their steel helmets; others standing by their lorries, with a piece of broken glass reared against the lorry, shaving in an empty jam tin. They used to get hot water from the lorry's radiator; and there were clothes hung up inside, evidently washed with water from the same source. Some were singing and whistling merrily and called a cheery, "Good evening, Sisters," as we passed along.

Péronne, too, was very badly smashed, but we could see what a beautiful town it once had been. We passed through Péronne and at about seven-thirty, reached Doingt. German signs hung everywhere and it was plain to see that the Germans had not long left this part, as there was evidence of their stay everywhere. 'Verboten', meaning 'forbidden', was a very familiar sign.

The Officer in charge of the convoy had received orders at Péronne for us to report at 55 CCS at Doingt. It was quite dark when we arrived there and we had great difficulty in finding our way, as we were not allowed any lights. Every now and then we were able to get a good view of the road from the guns at the firing line. This was always a wonderful sight to me. Often in camp on night duty, when the darkness used to make itself felt, we were guided on our rounds of the wards by the constant light from the guns. It was a pretty sight to see those flashes of light in the sky. We could always tell when there was a heavy barrage and often stood out on the duckboards watching, fascinated and horrified, wondering how many each shell was killing.

Supper was just being served at 55CCS when we arrived. Matron greeted us and told us she did not know where she would put us to sleep, as everywhere was already congested, sisters having come down from Tincourt from the various CCS there on account of the German shelling. They had put a shell in the reception room of one of the CCS and the colonel in charge had thought it better for the sisters to go to a place of safety for the night, for by morning they would have driven the Boche sufficiently back to prevent him from damaging the CCS. This was the reason we had not finished our journey.

After supper we went to a bell tent that Matron had had erected for us and prepared for sleep. We all slept soundly until morning. The staff of 55 CCS were all, what we called 'dug in', in their bell tents. Their beds were put into pits looking almost like graves. This was a great precaution against falling splinters.

A very heavy frost had fallen during the night, and it was cold dressing in that tent – the grass striking very cold to our feet. Most of us were not able to find water to wash in, so just went to breakfast as we were. About ten o'clock we started for Tincourt. The fighting all around here must have been terrible. Everything was destroyed and there was mound after mound of earth with a little cross bearing the name of a fallen hero, German, Belgian French, American and British – some with their steel helmet on top of the cross. It was a pitiful sight. They had evidently been buried just where they had fallen.

Again we passed our boys shaving, washing and drilling, but always with a cheery, "Good morning, Sister." Huge dumps of shells and shell cases, and boxes of cordite were everywhere on that battlefield – a great part of it belonging to the Germans, who had retreated so quickly they had no time to destroy or take it with them. We passed German prisoners of war who were clearing and mending roads. Some would glare at us, others smiled, but the majority would just look stolidly at us, not seeming to care for anything.

I often asked the prisoners I was nursing if they minded being taken prisoner, and they mostly replied that they preferred it to fighting but hoped that they would go home quickly after the war. They said the food and clothing we gave them were much better than they had received in the German Army and cigarettes were almost a thing of the past.

Arriving at 58 CCS, we found our officers having breakfast. They had only arrived a few hours before us and had already put up bell tents for sleeping and the reception marquee. Others were rapidly being erected. We were invited by our Colonel to have a second breakfast, which we did. Afterwards our bell tent was put up so we were able to get our beds up and then get our mess in order for the arrival of the remainder of the staff.

After dinner the Colonel told us one sister had better go to bed for night duty, and the other two to work in the reception room, as we were taking in the overflow from the CCS across from us. By this time, marquees were in every direction and soon the patients commenced to arrive. They were dressed by us in the reception marquee and passed on to the other marquees, which were being used as wards. We had soon admitted over three hundred, and still they came; everywhere was soon full to overflowing with patients. We were very thankful when [*the*] night sister came and took over, relieving us for the night. Thoroughly tired out, we had dinner and went to bed.

The next day passed in very much the same way. We had no time to think of anything, as patients were flowing in all the time. Shells were going over us with their mournful shriek; followed by their 'krupp...' all day long, but we were too busy to notice.

I was dressing a young Yankee boy in the evening and asked, "Are you wounded badly, sonny?"

He answered, "Yes, Sir." Then laughed and corrected himself, "Yes, Ma'am," followed by "Gee Whiz, it's the first woman I've seen for months and then I go and call her 'Sir'!" The officer standing by joined in the laugh; he, too, was an American.

This boy had been sent down from Bellicourt. We asked him how things were and he said his battalion had almost been cut off by the Germans. Somehow or other they had missed the Bellicourt Tunnel, where the Germans were, in their thousands. The battalion had driven all the Germans out of the area and were following them up country, when the Germans in the tunnel started to come out after them. Had not the Australians, who were also in that vicinity, come to their assistance, they would all have been taken prisoner.

About ten o'clock that night our dressing tent was looking an awful mess; blood-stained dressings lying almost knee-deep on the floor, splints and parts of kits lying everywhere; and we had used up our stock of dressings, so we decided to call a rest and clear up to get it all ready for the night duty. There were still a hundred or so, mostly Germans, waiting for dressings. We knew that meant the end of an offensive, as the Germans were always sent in last. After about an hour everything was cleared and the new dressings piled up, awaiting the next onslaught.

It was almost midnight before we got to bed that night. We went to sleep very easily, but not for long. A storm arose – very heavy wind and rain. We heard our tent moaning and creaking against its bearings and wondered how long it would keep up. Very soon we felt the canvas flapping across our faces and the rain began to beat in. Voices seemed to be everywhere in the darkness. Then someone came around our tent and fixed the cords and pegs, asking us if we were all right. We told them yes; too tired to worry much. I am afraid if the old tent had blown away, which it very nearly did, we would still have tried to find sleep and protection in our beds in the open! The storm raged all night long, and we constantly heard the men pegging us in; but we managed to get a little sleep in between times.

Morning came, with its rush of wounded, and we worked well into the night once more; getting up in the morning feeling very weary with so little sleep, but to find the remainder of the staff, who had been on duty since three a.m., ready to give a helping hand. Sisters were detailed to the various wards and the operating theatre was put in readiness. Then the work started properly; Colonel told us we had taken in nine hundred patients during those three days whilst we were alone.

It was arranged that one surgical team should work in the dressing room each day, and then operate in the evening, provided all the cases had been seen. This made it very hard, as we would often be in the dressing room until nine p.m. and doing operations until one, two, three or possibly four a.m., managing with as little sleep as possible. For a fortnight we worked like this. Oh, how weary we got, but we did not feel it so much when we were working. It was when we came to get up in the morning after so little sleep that we felt it the most. Our eyes simply would not open and we staggered about for about an hour, like someone under the influence of drink or drugs.

Several of the CCS from across the way had moved by this time, following the advancing boys, so this made our work a little lighter; and it got progressively lighter each day, so that we were able to get a little off-duty time and made up our lost sleep. The shells by this time had stopped screaming over us and the air-raids, what few we had, amounted to very little.

Some Australians, billeted round about, had built the sisters dug-outs, to protect us from any falling shrapnel. These dug-outs were wonderfully made, being about 6 ft. deep, 8 ft. wide and 10 ft. long. They were made of heavy beams of wood driven into the ground, with corrugated iron nailed to these. This formed the sides and roof. The floor was also planked. There were two shelves on either side of the dug-out, a window in the far end, with another shelf underneath, which we used as a dressing table, and a nice little stove in the corner by the door, with a bag of coal and wood all ready to start our fire.

The window and door windows were made of cream-coloured oiled cloth, which gave us plenty of light, though we could not see out of it. The outside of the dug-out was covered with sandbags, and four steps led down into the dug-out from a wired duckboard walk above. Two sisters shared a dug-out, and we were very comfortable, especially so when we got our little stoves going. The Australians had named each dug-out. Ours was called 'Bullie Villa', others, 'Anzac Villa', 'Welcome Cottage', 'Australian Heights' etc.

The Australians were very good to us whilst they were billeted near. I remember once we ran out of oatmeal for porridge and in the morning a huge sack of oatmeal arrived, with the Aussies' compliments. Furniture of every description they showered on us too, taken from the various devastated homes around. These days we were living strictly on army rations, as the nearest shopping centre was Amiens, seventy miles distant and all the army canteens were very poorly supplied around us. It became tiring, as it meant so much bully beef and pickles. Our cook often tried to camouflage the bully beef but we could always tell what it was.

As fewer patients came in, we were allowed our proper off-duty time – three hours a day. This we spent chiefly looking around the battlefields; walking through the trenches, dug-outs and various places sightseeing. All the killed soldiers had been buried by the clearing party, but the dead horses were still lying about. Poor things; they too, had paid the price of war. Shells, guns and warfare appliances were strewn everywhere. There surely had been a heavy battle there.

On a hill facing our CCS about fifteen minutes' walk away, was quite a village made of Nissen huts, occupied at that time by the Americans. This was quite a pretty spot, surrounded by trees which covered most of the huts. It was said to have been one of the German headquarters taken by the British, retaken by the Germans and finally by the British. It was a splendidly concealed spot and at night looked very pretty with its many twinkling lights.

We visited Longavesnes, Templeux-la-Fosse – all lying in ruins – dead cities. We often went to Templeux-la-Fosse to gather flowers. There were beautiful rose trees with the tops cut off, but bearing roses in spite of it all – truly 'Roses of Picardy'. There were also a few chrysanthemums and Michaelmas Daisies which we eagerly gathered.

Tincourt itself had been quite a nice town but, like the rest, it was lying in ruins. The church there seemed to be the only place that was standing and even that had one or two shells in it. Service was held there every Sunday night for the boys billeted round and about. We often went to this church and looked around the graveyard. Almost all the vaults had been opened. We looked down and saw the coffins destroyed and, in many cases, the skeletons of the ones who had been laid to rest taken out of the coffins and strewn about the floor. Every coffin, too, was stripped of its brass handles and plates. We were told the Germans had used these vaults during air raids and shell fire.

There were no civilians at all in this part of the country. Almost all had retreated – [*now*] refugees in some other part or captured by the Germans – so that we had to do our own washing. Usually we got some of the French or Belgium people to do it for us. Water was very scarce here too, so that made us very careful. Often I bathed, and then got my washing to soak overnight in the same water, managing to get clean water to rinse off at the end. It was no unusual thing for us those days to fill our hot water bottles at night, wash in that same water from the bottle and in the evening, boil it up to use it in our bottles again, and so on.

In the wards, too, we had to be very careful – several patients washing in the same water and very little of that. If we used it all for washing purposes there would be none left for the sick for drinking water. Water was brought every day to us in a water cart – I think from Péronne. Two water carts full was our ration, so you will understand it was very little for cooking, washing, operations etc., for the whole hospital and staff. This was relieved somewhat later by having a water supply laid on.

One day Matron came and asked me if I would like to go to Bellicourt, to the Hindenburg Line with two other sisters, in charge of some of our MOs. We assured her 'Yes', so after dinner we got ready. The ambulance that brought the mail daily was to take me. About one-thirty we climbed into the ambulance and were soon on our way. We passed the ruined beet sugar factory of Tincourt, soon arriving at Marquaix, where the army canteen, with its everlasting stream of khaki figures pouring in and out, buying what they could of its luxuries in those days, was stationed. Roisel came next, with its big railroad crossing. We received quite a number of wounded from Roisel; a delayed German mine exploding and killing several and wounding many.

At Templeux we saw quite a number of our boys. One picture we saw as we passed through Templeux always remains in my mind. A bunch of our boys were on a paved square of what had been a house, and a fragment of the inner wall with a fireplace still remained. This group of boys had built a fire and were sitting around it, smoking and chatting, enjoying the warm glow, even though it was raining as hard as it possibly could. There was an old tin on the fire with water in it, which they were boiling to make tea. They called cheerily to us and invited us to have tea with them.

Templeux, like every other town and village in this part of France, was one mass of debris. One building, which resembled a big farm house, had a huge red cross on part of the shelled wall, and written in German, 'First aid' and then, in English, 'British First Aid'. At one part of the road there were small hills running on either side; holes had been dug in the sides of these hills. These the Germans had used to store their ammunition, and it was now lying in great disorder everywhere. Disused tanks, guns and aeroplanes were lying all over and [it] did not seem there was one square inch of ground that had not been shelled.

Some of the huge craters were almost full of water. I wondered, as we passed this, how many of the boys had lost their lives in those filthy, stagnant pools. We could see dug-outs and trenches of every description for miles, and as we raced along, we saw in the distance, miles and miles of barbed wire, row after row, field after field.

At the entrance of Hargicourt stood a lone crucifix, as though guarding the town. The town itself was pitiful to see – not a building standing, not even a part. How that crucifix had remained standing was ever a marvel to me. It must have been the hand of God, giving those who were fighting for right and freedom, courage and a message: 'Be ye not afraid – Lo, I am with you always.'

Some of the fiercest fighting must have taken place here. Ground gained, retaken and regained. The ground was just simply torn up, and as we passed along, about two miles before we reached Bellicourt, the road was made of heavy sleepers. Our driver told us that every inch of this road had been so heavily mined, shelled and bombed, it had been impossible to repair it any other way. One huge mine-hole they had never been able to cover, so they had made a circle around it of the sleepers. In this way, the in-going traffic could use one road and the out-going the other, without danger of running into one another, and so prevent themselves getting drowned, as the hole was full of water.

We found this road very tiring and difficult to travel over, and we had to hang on to the car to keep from being thrown out. It was on this road that we saw some Australians with one of the big 'Bouncing Bertha' guns, which they had captured from the Germans, being pulled by a German lorry. That must have been a very rough journey for those Aussies as the German lorry had no rubber tyres. They had just plain iron wheels – the Germans having no rubber in those days.

We passed through miles and miles of barbed wire of the Hindenburg Line, and were soon at Bellicourt – a city of white dust, from constant bombardment of the Allies and the Germans.[16] Here we left the ambulance, which proceeded on its way to Estrées for the mail. It was to stop at Bellicourt on its way back to pick us up.

Descending a hill which was almost hidden by the road, we came to the canal side. This canal was absolutely hidden by the high hills on either side. Huts and dug-outs of every description were everywhere on the hillside, giving the appearance of a town on the hill by the river. Small wooden bridges spanned the canal at intervals. It was on one of these small bridges that two of our boys – a private and a corporal – won the Victoria Cross for bravery, holding the Germans back and preventing them crossing the bridge.[17]

We noticed the water was very still and clear, with not a ripple to be seen. Hundreds of steel helmets – German, French, Belgian, British and American – were lying in the bottom, showing the number who must have fallen in during the heavy fighting. Some, perhaps, with only slight wounds that would just have drowned; others may have been dead before they reached the water. Guns, bayonets, gas-masks, shells, cartridges, and, it seemed, almost every implement of war were lying there.

We passed through the mouth of the Bellicourt Tunnel – a tunnel seven miles long, said to have been built by Napoleon with the aid of Russian prisoners, years ago. The Germans had cemented the mouths of the tunnel, bottling up in the canal, hundreds of barges belonging to the French – hence the stillness of the water.

A flight of stone stairs led up to a long narrow room on one side of the canal. This room had two big iron cauldrons in it, full of yellow fat. Two big wheels, with a long narrow trough leading to these boilers, were fixed in the centre of the room. We heard that this was where the Germans used to make glycerine from their dead, and our boys have said, "Not only theirs, but those of the Allies too."

It is supposed, when this tunnel was taken over by the British, that stacks and stacks of dead were piled in fours in this room, and that hands, feet and skulls were piled in heaps, covered with chloride of lime; also, that a German, leaning over one of the cauldrons, was headless, his head floating in the fat. This fat was supposed to have been analysed and found to contain human fat. For my part, I do not think this gruesome, terrible story is true. I think the dead, stacked in rows of fours, must have been collected from the tunnel and the German by the cauldron must have had his head shot off, although that room did not show any sign of fighting.

Descending the stone stairway, we came across another small room and waded through thousands, no, millions of cartridges, almost ankle deep; evidently a storeroom. Passing further into the tunnel, we saw the huge black forms of the barges, looking very gruesome in the candle light, which we had thoughtfully brought with us. We put out lights down into the opening and saw rows of bunks, similarly built to those on a train or ship, but of course not so luxurious. They were made of posts of wood and wire netting such as is used for hen coops, etc. These were used by the Germans as beds. There was furniture of every description, which they had looted from the French, placed so as to make the place as much like home as possible.

Almost all the barges had two or three feet of water in them. We passed further into the tunnel and noticed that the Germans had filled part of the canal to make a sidewalk, extending from the tunnel side to the barges. About a mile into the tunnel, we came across a small house of four rooms, built right over the water. There was no furniture in the house, but a bathroom fixed up with a beautiful porcelain bath and, about halfway up the wall, a pale blue wooden beading running all around. The doors were painted blue and white. These decorations, and the bath, evidently belonged to some French house. It had been a very nice place, but now was terribly battered. Next to this small house on the water was a big barge fitted up as an electric shop, with every kind of electric appliance.

Across from this house on the water, were four rooms built right into the side of the hill from the tunnel. The walls were made of stone. One room had an engine in it, which had been stripped of every bit of brass and copper. This engine had something to do with the lighting of the tunnel, or water-power, I don't know which. Another room on the opposite side of the little hallway had also been used as an electrical shop. All manner of wires and different appliances hung on the wall and in the room next to this were heaps of empty bottles, in openings in the walls, on shelves and also on a centre bench with shelves leading right up to the ceiling. This was obviously one of the German wine cellars. In the fourth room there were tubs of yellow fat.

Everywhere in the tunnel showed heavy fighting; guns, bayonets and shells being thick upon the floor. Several notices in English with 'Don't Touch' or 'Danger' were placed at intervals along the tunnel. There were also different openings leading to the trenches above. We decided to go out by one of these openings, just to see what it was like. How our legs ached by the time we had mounted those steps – 132 in all. We noticed huge, thick pipes, like those used in this country [*America*] for stoves, travelling up the side of the wall leading from the tunnel to the trenches. These were to carry fresh air into the tunnel. There were also doors at intervals, the length of the stairway. When a gas attack was on, these were tightly secured, making all entrance of gas impossible.

We reached the top of the steps and were thankful for the fresh air again. The opening was completely hidden by a wall of sand bags. Twice afterwards I made this trip with other sisters and found a fresh entrance every time; once going into the tunnel through a ruined house; another time, in the trenches again but a different spot.

One time I went out with two sisters, confident I could find my way again, but somehow or other I missed the road. The roads seemed all alike in this devastated shell-wrecked land, and it was very easy to get lost. We found ourselves right out in No-Man's Land – not a soul in sight – and we did not know which way to turn. The stillness was horrible. No wonder human beings go mad when shipwrecked on some desert island. For about two miles we tramped through trenches, dug-outs and craters; it was only as dusk was beginning to fall that we noticed a road. We decided to take it and return in the direction we had come. All at once I saw what looked to be a soldier; so, hurrying as fast as we could, we approached him. I was just going to ask the way to Bellicourt, when I noticed that it was a faked German.

The clearing party had been out gathering together shells, guns etc., and from this pile of guns they had made this German figure. They had stuck two guns into the ground and tied another one across, by adding trousers, tunic and a steel helmet they had completed the figure. We laughed heartily, but were just a bit anxious, not wishing to spend the night out in No-Man's Land. However, after about another mile or so we came across a devastated town which seemed to be familiar; we realised it was Bellicourt. Boarding lorries, we were soon on our way home to Tincourt.

About half a mile from our camp was the little village of Boucly. It was here that Hennessy, of the Hennessy Three Star Brandy had a very big château, standing in its own grounds of a few acres. The château had been occupied by the Germans. After their retreat our advancing army, needing billets, sent an officer in charge of a number of men to investigate. The officer approached the château, raised the knocker on the door, and there followed a terrible explosion, killing the officer and every soldier with him. Some were just blown to fragments and could not be found. The château became just one pile of loose stones.

We often went around this place and one day we noticed several tanks in the grounds. It was not long before we were talking to the officers in charge and they showed us inside the tanks. We found it very interesting, but decided we would rather be out in the open during an offensive, than fastened up in one of those death traps with their hundreds of shells and guns. We fancied ourselves in there when a shell hit one, or one of their own shells exploded. Well, death would come so quickly and so surely, we would not know.

One of these Tank Corps officers came up one Sunday afternoon and said he would take us for a ride. We had heard a rumour that the sister in charge had forbidden us to go, but we decided to close our ears. She had not told us herself and we wanted so much to take that ride in the tank! So, in we climbed and the driver started the engine. Soon we were on our way. What a racket inside that tank. I wonder the boys could stand it! We had to shout at the top of our voices, with our hands hollowed around our mouths, into the other's ear, and even then found it difficult to hear.

We thought that the tank was going at least twenty-five or thirty miles an hour, but on looking through the little peep holes, we found we were just crawling along with another officer walking leisurely by the side. The driver told us we were going just four miles an hour! The fumes in the tank from the engine soon began to worry us and we sneezed and coughed, with our eyes streaming. During an offensive the officer told us they carried pigeons to carry messages, but the fumes from the engine often killed them.

We were informed they would do no stunts with the sisters inside, but they took one or two small embankments and turned around occasionally. One embankment was very steep – it seemed we would stand on our heads. The driver turned round on the top and commenced to come down. Then we saw all the equipment on the top of the tank starting to fall down, and not only this, but human beings too. We got close up to the driver and yelled, "There's a man underneath!" He put on his brakes with all possible haste, but it seemed some little time before the tank came to a standstill. The driver's face was pallid and we felt ours were too.

Hastily jumping from the tank, we learned it was the Padre who had fallen off, and that he had been taken to the officers' ward with a crushed skull. Terrified, we ran to our wards or operating rooms, wherever we were working, and were hard at work when Matron came in. She looked very keenly at us and asked if we had heard about the Padre? We replied that we had heard, but she did not ask if we had been in the tank. We then asked her how the Padre was and if he was seriously wounded. She told us he had a very nasty scalp wound, but apparently no bones had been broken.

We heard afterwards that Matron knew unofficially that we were in the tank, but she never questioned us. In the evening we asked permission to visit the Padre to try to console him. He was classed as a self-inflicted. He looked very pale, his white bandage accentuating the whiteness of his face; otherwise, so he informed us, he felt all right.

A medical officer was sick with the flu, so we visited him at the same time. They were in beds next to one another. Seated at the end of the officer's bed was another medical officer whom I had never seen before. He never spoke or greeted us in any way and when I got outside I asked the Sisters who he was. They told me he was Mr Aylen, an American Lieutenant, who had joined up with the Canadian Forces before America had come into the War; he had then been transferred into the British Army Medical Corps. He had just returned from leave and was the X-ray Specialist for 58 Casualty Clearing Station.

I said, "What a solemn looking man," and did not think he looked very sociable. They informed me he was very reserved, but very nice; but if I could make him talk then I would have worked wonders! I met him often after that, was introduced, and often he used to play my [*piano*] accompaniments when I was singing.

(I did not find it difficult to converse with him ever, and you will well know, when I tell you that I am now his wife and this minute, as I write in our own dear little home, he is sitting at the other side of the table, reading, unaware that the scratch-scratch of my pen is telling of our meeting. They call me a 'War Bride' and truly that is so, as we met right out on the battle-fields in 'No-Man's Land'!)

Peace and Romance: 9 November 1918 – 14 December 1918
On November 9th we were awakened by a loud rat-tat on our dug-out door, and heard the cry: "Sister, Sister, the Germans have asked for an Armistice. We have them on the run and our troops are following them up

with machine guns in lorries, or tied to motorcycles, or anything else they could fasten them to."

We just grunted and wondered, 'Why, oh why, would they not let us sleep – disturbing us in this way!' The night sister went away in disgust because we were too sleepy to take notice. I remember, as I turned over on my camp bed, thinking, 'Too good to be true', although it had been terribly quiet everywhere for some time and we had thought the Boche must be planning some new offensive. We did not trust him, but the next morning we were told it was true and that, Tuesday, the 11th November, had been fixed for the signing of the Armistice.

November 11th, 1918, dawned clear and fair, but with stillness everywhere. The roads around our camp were lined with lorries – all awaiting orders. Everyone seemed under a spell. The boys in our wards spoke in whispers, as though something mighty was going to happen, and when we spoke to them about the Armistice, they said, "Oh Sister; it is too good to be true; we know the Boche better than anybody. He is planning something fresh; that is why he wants an Armistice. We ought not to give them one." Many remarks were heard such as this one.

Midday came and still nothing happened. Then about twelve-fifteen we heard sirens, loud clapping, cheering and big explosions of shells which the Aussies were setting off. They had made a bonfire of cordite into which they were putting the shells, before running off as fast as they could. Even then my boys would not cheer up and it was not until my Medical Officer came around and said orders had gone round for hostilities to cease at eleven a.m. that my boys believed it to be true. I turned to them and said, "Now boys, you can cheer." Which they did [*whole*]heartedly. We celebrated the occasion with pieces of dry cake, broken biscuits and coffee, but the boys enjoyed it as much as though it had been a big dinner at the Savoy in London.

The personnel celebrated a few nights afterwards with a dinner and concert at which I sang, Mr Aylen playing my accompaniment. Then we had a dinner in the officers' mess. This was not really allowed but we felt justified on such an occasion as this. Everything on the menu was, in war terms, very cleverly done but I am sorry to say that I have lost my copy.

Colonel told us after dinner that he had seen the DMS Army (Director of the Medical Services 4th Army) and that out of the five CCS that were at Tincourt, four were to follow the advancing troops, staying about a week or fortnight at a time in one place. How we hoped our CCS might be one of the lucky ones to follow our boys in that march of victory, but we were all doomed to disappointment when a few days later we received orders to remain where we were. Our CCS was to be used as a self-inflicted hospital and for sick troops billeted round and about. Colonel told us the DMS 4th Army had told him our CCS had done wonderful work and he regretted we were the ones to remain, but that someone had to stay and we were the ones chosen.

My ward was a self-inflicted ward. They were all classed as self-inflicted until they had had their trial. Some of them were purely accidental cases, such as petrol burns, fractures from stumbling down a crater, but some were true self-inflicted, as shot-off fingers and toes. They thought it would hurry their departure home, but it only lengthened the time [*before*] they would see England.

One boy I had in one day had his nose knocked on to the side of his face. He looked so funny! He told me that he and his pal had nothing better to do and were throwing bricks at one another. One had apparently caught him on the nose, which resulted in the mess. He was operated on that night and his nose put back as near to the original place as they possibly could, but he would always carry a crooked nose.

We had a mixture in the wards these days – British, American and Indians. The Indians were funny. They would eat nothing but rice and drink milk. It was very hard, not knowing just what to give them. They carried a hammered brass bowl with them all the time. I wanted one very much as a souvenir, but my boys told me if I dared to take one my life would be in danger, as it was part of their religion. I noticed letters and figures in Hindustani engraved all around the bowls. They used them to eat, drink and wash out of; and kept them spotlessly clean.

Impromptu concerts were arranged very often to amuse the boys, as they were more discontented after the Armistice than ever before, wondering why they could not immediately return home to their loved ones. Well, I remember one night we received an invitation from the Padre to one of these concerts, which was supposed to be at eight p.m. We waited about an hour, but none of the artists had arrived, so Padre came over and asked me if I would mind giving them a song. I gave them 'When you Come Home, Dear' and for my encore 'There's a Long, Long Trail A-Winding'.

By this time the boys who had been hiding at the back of the marquee began to come out and do their bit. They were dressed in pyjamas and were supposed to be wrestlers, but they turned out to be boxers, and in earnest too. One yelled to the other, "What did you hit me like that for, d–you?" And the other, "Fight, d– you!" So they were turned outside to finish, much to the amusement of all of us. After that episode several of the officers gave readings, so we enjoyed the concert after all.

Often trips for shopping were made into Amiens, about seventy miles distant and we sisters used to take it in turns to go. We often passed Villers-Carbonnel a town flattened to the ground, [*and*] upon this sign someone had added, 'This *was* Villers-Carbonnel'. Nothing else remained to tell what it had been. We passed through Estrées, Herville, Ramecourt and Lamotte. We saw a Zeppelin which had been brought down in 1914, lying on the side of the road, looking like the carcass of some huge monster. All this ground we passed through was torn up, skulls of horses lying everywhere and the churches and villages one heap of ruins.

Between Warfusée and Villers-Bretonneux very fierce fighting must have taken place – more fierce than at other places, if that were possible.[18] There were small hills and valleys everywhere. One valley had been called the 'Valley of Death'. It is said that the fiercest fighting took place here, and truly it looked as though it had. Huge stacks of ammunition of every description were piled in dumps, guns and bayonets in high stacks and on the side of the road, under the embankment were little white crosses, where the boys had been buried where they had fallen, one by one. I cannot describe to you the horror of it all, although it is so clear in my mind. One had to see it to realize.

One time we were round by Bray [*Bray-sur-Somme*], thinking to cut off a few miles, but the road we went on had been very heavily shelled and had not been repaired. The shell holes were half-full of water and our car got stuck in one. It took the driver and the officer with us an hour to get it out. We went off and gathered mushrooms growing by a wrecked aeroplane which had been lying there some little time, or so it looked.

As we reached Amiens, we passed a field full of German guns, very heavily camouflaged, which we had captured. All the trees along the road from Tincourt to Amiens were broken off – lifeless, as though some heavy tempest had raged. They had all been destroyed by the shells.

Once when we passed along this road, we met a column of Australians who were going to march into Germany as part of the Army Victorious. The sun was sinking in the West, and I thought what a beautiful picture it made. The officers, men and horses were so neatly groomed; all wearing their bronze badge, 'The Rising Sun', and the roseate reflection of the setting sun covered them with its glorious hue. If only an artist could have seen that picture, I am sure he would have called it 'The Rising and the Setting Sun'. [*Here in her manuscript Beatrice quotes 'Ambition' by Jay M. Aitch.*[19]]

About half a mile from Tincourt, on the way to Longavene [*possibly Longueval*], was a small grove, trenches running in every direction. Dug-outs built in the sides of these trenches were in great number, the trees forming a good shelter. Just outside this grove were three disused tanks, very badly battered – two British and one French. We often used to go over and look at these. Their sides were blown out and there were pieces of shells and machinery lying all around. Written on the side, in chalk, was 'captured by Germans, retaken by French; again captured by Germans and retaken by French; again captured by the Germans and retaken by the British,' with all the dates of the individual captures. The boys inside those tanks must have been blown to dust, as almost everything in and about the tanks was.

Sleep, in our dug-outs, those nights was almost impossible, owing to the many rats making their homes round and about. Often during the night we would feel a heavy thud on our beds and hear a squeal from a rat which had found its way into our dug-out and fallen off the shelf. I believe I hated those monsters more than bombs. Some of them were as big as a good sized kitten.

Matron had our dispenser make up some rat poison, which was put around the dug-out and any place where the rats would be likely to be; but the noise still went on and we had them visiting us every night. Personnel collected all the stray dogs around the camp (which were many) and removed a few of the sand-bags from each dug-out. Soon enough started a scampering, squealing and barking. How those dogs enjoyed the hunt and ever after, one had only to say "Rats," and the dogs would race *en masse* to the dug-outs. They used to hunt every other day, which meant the rats did not have much of a chance to billet with us again.

On November 29th, 1918, my leave came through. I did not want my leave at that time, but I had to go. Two other sisters were also going on leave and we had to pack very hastily. Whenever we went on leave, we had to take all our heavy luggage and leave it at the base, as it was very seldom we ever returned to the camp we had left.[20] The officers came into our mess that night to say goodbye. Well I remember how gloomy we all felt at leaving; we were all so happy there.

At seven o'clock the next morning we boarded the lorry and away we went to Amiens to catch the train en route for Boulogne. We arrived in Amiens about eleven a.m., very tired and cold. We saw our luggage registered and learned that the train did not leave until three p.m., so found a restaurant serving lunch, after which we felt very refreshed and then returned to the station in time to catch the train. Arriving at the station, we learned from the RTO (Railway Transport Officer) that our train had already left at midday and that it was the troop train leaving at three p.m. No sisters were allowed to travel on that, but we persuaded him to let us board the troop train.

Punctually at three, we boarded that troop train and managed to get into what had been a first class compartment, and which now was only fit for the scrap heap. There were no cushions on the seats and only remnants of the upholstering on the back of the seats. The door had been torn away and three pieces of white board were nailed across in its place. A tattered piece of canvas hung as a blind. The windows were in the same condition. We made ourselves as comfortable as possible and wrapped ourselves in the extra coats, as the wind just whistled through those partly boarded apertures. It was so cold.

Several officers were in the compartment and they were very good to us, giving us some of their refreshments they had brought along with them. They had already been on the train for two days and were just tired of it, longing for Boulogne where they could find rest and have a good clean up. It soon began to grow dusk and we thought we were in for a very dismal time, but those boys had come prepared and produced candles which they lighted. Turning the candle upside down, they let some of the tallow fall on that once first class window ledge, sticking the candle in this to make it stand. It was only a feeble glow, but very welcome. A candle out in France was always an officer's, Tommy's and sister's friend.

We passed the time by telling stories and singing songs. At one station we had to wait about an hour. Those boys went out in search of a canteen, which they found some little distance away, and returned within half an hour, laden with condensed milk, cans filled with tea and a number of packages of biscuits. When safely inside, one of the boys pulled a YMCA cup out of his pocket. He said they would not give him one, so he had helped himself. The tea, which was already cold, but refreshing, was passed around and we settled ourselves for another two or three hours' ride. The candle was blown out and we all went to sleep, awaking to find ourselves at Boulogne and it almost midnight.

After seeing our luggage safely stored, we walked across the quay to the Hotel Du Nord, about fifteen minutes' walk from the station. Arriving at the hotel, we noticed it was in almost complete darkness, but it was not long before a light was switched on in answer to our summons and a head thrust out of an upper window enquiring "Who is there?" We were soon admitted, supper given to us and tucked away in our beds.

The Hotel Du Nord was run by the Canadians and it truly was a comfort to stay there. It lacked the restrained feeling one had in our own hostels. Notices were not placed everywhere, with a list of 'Don'ts' everlastingly before one's eyes. I am sure every English sister and VAD used to fight to get into that hotel when passing through Boulogne. The food also was much better than we received in our hostels. I do not know why, unless because of the rationing in England and I think the Canadians provided almost all their own food for this hostel, so perhaps that may have been the reason.

Punctually at nine a.m. the morning boat left Boulogne Harbour and we were soon on our way across the choppy Channel to our dear old Blighty. The boys with whom we had travelled from Amiens in the troop train were on the boat and had deckchairs reserved for us in a sheltered spot. They were very good to us and when we arrived back in England took us across London in taxis to the station, where our train was leaving for the Midlands.

I arrived in Nottingham about seven p.m., where my two sisters, Gertrude and Doris, excitedly met me; it was not long before I was home. But my leave soon passed. I travelled to London and met up with one of the sisters whom I had travelled home with. We went to a show together, after which we separated, meeting again in the afternoon to catch our train en route for France.

By this time we had gotten used to the crossing and seemed to have no fear of sea-sickness or torpedoes, and the time passed very quickly. We were soon in Boulogne again, at the Hotel Du Nord, awaiting orders and hoping all the time we would be sent back to 58 CCS.

Namur, Belgium: 14 December 1918 – May 1919

The next morning, 14th December, 1918, we received orders to report with all our heavy luggage to the nurses' home at Abbeville, another quaint town of France. Here we waited four days, then received orders to return to the Hotel Du Nord, Boulogne. Arriving there we were told we were to await the ambulance train going up to Germany and that we were to go to Namur. How our hearts sank. We had so wanted to go back to 58 CCS. For two days we waited in Boulogne, then on the 20th December, 1918, we boarded the Ambulance Train for Namur, Belgium.[21]

The train left Wimereux Siding about seven in the evening. We were given the isolation coach and the officers' dining coach for a sitting and dining room. An English officer was in charge of the Ambulance Train, along with three Australian sisters and the personnel. They were running between Cologne, Germany and Boulogne. Usually on the journey to Cologne the train was empty, unless taking sisters up to various CCS along the route, as in our case. This was only allowed after the Armistice. There were about thirty of us, all going to different CCS; some to Charleroi, some Namur, Huy and Cologne.

It took us two days to reach Namur and it was about midnight when we arrived.[22] We were so thankful too, to get off that train, as our clothing was covered with 'chats' [*lice*]. I believe I must have gotten fifty off one sleeve of my vest alone. All the sisters were the same, and some had even got them in their hair. It was a funny sight to see each sister every night whilst on the train (and I guess, judging by ourselves, for many nights afterwards) sitting as near to the light as possible, hunting for those 'night hawks'. It reminded me very much of the Tommies sitting by the candle, hunting.

I am afraid we never put them back and gave them a home for life, like the Tommy who was standing on the parapet when he felt a bite. Hastening into the trench, he looked into his shirt and found a cootie. Whilst he was thus engaged, a shell came over and fell almost exactly where he had been standing. Death would have been certain. He looked at the cootie, then at the spot where the shell had fallen, and finally he put the cootie back where he found it, with these words, "Well, old pal, you surely have saved my life; you can go back where I found you and have a home for life!"

These chats were terrible and, try as one might, one could not keep free of them. We used to get them whilst kneeling on the floor, doing dressings of the patients on stretchers and in many other ways; always hunting at night, one sister saying to the other, "Any luck tonight?" One could only make light of it all.

I saw a very sad thing whilst at 58 CCS at Tincourt. A patient was admitted in an unconscious state. When we came to take off his shirt, it was simply covered with chats. One could not have put a pin head in a vacant spot and when the shirt was taken off and placed outside to be burned, one could not tell whether it was the shirt or the cooties moving but move it did. It was a horrible sight.

The boy himself was in a very poor state of anaemia, caused through those animals sucking his blood. History related the patient as unsound of mind, with insufficient sense to hunt these cooties, hence his state. Poor boy, he only lived a few hours after admission; his body was too covered with bites to survive. [*Here in the manuscript Beatrice quotes 'Idle Moments in the Line', by Jay M. Aitch.*]

We reported at the orderly room in the station, where the sergeant in charge telephoned the 48 CCS to let them know of our arrival. We were told to leave our kits at the station and proceed to the hospital, accompanied by one of the men out of the orderly room. When we got out into the cobbled streets of Namur, with its many brick buildings, we noticed flags in great array. We were told by the Tommy with us that they had been hoisted when the Armies Victorious passed through on their triumphal march to Cologne.

48 CCS was about five minutes' walk from the station, so we were soon in the presence of the night sisters who gave us refreshment. We then went to bed in the sick sisters' quarters, which was also a part of 48 CCS, not waking until we were called about seven o'clock the next morning. When we were ready, we went with the night sisters in the Duty Ambulance to the Nurses' Home in another part of the town, about a ten minute walk from the hospital.

The Nurses' Home was a large brick building, used during the German invasion by the German WAACS (Women's Auxiliary Army Corps and Service).[23] It was beautifully fitted up with furniture of every description taken from the many shops in the town.

After breakfast we saw the sister in charge of 48 CCS and she told me I would be for night duty that night, and would not be needed during the day; so after getting my bed made up and things ready for the night duty, I went with another night sister to explore the town. Namur is a beautiful city, lying in a valley; its citadel standing on a hill overlooking the town like some big sentinel. When up at the top of the citadel, on a clear day, one can see for miles and miles around, getting a very pretty view with the many hills and dales and winding water-ways.

The Cathedral of Namur is a wonderful building, not of the French type with their many turrets and carvings, but something more massive and stately. Inside the cathedral too, was very impressive. There was not the tawdry finery, hangings, etc., as so often seen in the French churches, but a more stately and grand appearance with its many stone pillars, tiled floors, huge dome of glass and many beautiful paintings.

About midday we decided to go back to the Home to try to get a little sleep before our night duty. But sleep was impossible, owing to the constant traffic over the cobbled streets. After dinner, which was always at seven-thirty p.m. (the first sitting), we climbed into the duty ambulance and went to the hospital. I was given several small wards, holding from six to thirty patients. Almost all were influenza cases and some of them were very ill indeed and needed constant attention. As time went on we became very busy. The influenza was spreading rapidly and the boys were dying in threes and fours nightly. It became terrible – much more so now that the War was ended; to think that those poor boys, after going through what they had, being smitten in that way.

Christmas drew near and the Belgian people showered loads of holly and mistletoe on us. They had heard that the English people always decorated their homes at Christmas and intended we should have as much a 'home Christmas' in a strange land as possible. We used all we could and even then, for days afterwards, big piles stood in the corners of the corridors.

On Christmas Day the Belgian people gave us a concert and all the patients who could possibly go were allowed to attend. There was a string band which played some very good selections, and one or two singers whom we did not understand, but found very amusing, owing to their weird gesticulations. After the concert, and as we filed out of the theatre, each Tommy, officer and sister was presented with a small parcel, tied up with ribbon in the Belgian colours, with a sprig of holly and mistletoe. These parcels contained gifts such as photo frames, purses, paper knives, made out of pieces of shrapnel, greeting cards etc., and were given by the Belgian Red Cross.

We were informed [*that*] tea was being served in the officers' mess. There was plenty of ham, egg, cucumber and salmon sandwiches, and cakes, big and small, in great array. Before very long they had all been consumed but were replaced repeatedly. Two orderlies were busy preparing the food and in a little while I saw the officers had a look of anxiety on their faces. They were wondering, would they have enough to satisfy [*us*]? It was the best thing we sisters had seen for a long time. We tried to hide in the corners to cover our laughing faces and some to mop their tears, their mirth was so great. I think the colonel and officers would never invite a crowd of Belgians for tea again. They ate that day's rations and [*rations for*] three more. The poor officers had to go out into town to buy more food. Instead of afternoon tea, they made it their evening meal.

During the Christmas week, we night people were awakened by the 'Scotties', with their bagpipes. They had been invited by our Matron to tea and brought out the full band. We watched them swing along – their kilts swaying in unison. It is a beautiful sight to see a kilted regiment. There is something so fascinating about it that somehow warms your heart. They formed a circle in front of the Hostel and played for almost half an hour. By that time the crowd had become so dense they had to move off to allow the traffic to pass.

After tea there was a concert given by the Scotties. One Scottie gave a Highland Fling; another a sword dance, singing recitations and an officer cartoonist finished the programme. This Officer was really very clever. His Colonel was sitting by our Matron and was looking very happy as he chatted to Matron, who was also a Scot. Jock, the artist, thought he would have a joke and sketched his Colonel just as he was looking whilst answering Matron. Then he sketched Matron as she spoke to the Colonel; everyone in the theatre laughed heartily.

My night duty passed along very quickly and it was not very long before I was on day duty, in charge of two huts, holding about thirty patients in each. These huts were used for acute influenza cases. I will never forget that month. I had thirty-five deaths in less than a month – patients dying every day. Oh, it was terrible! How hard I worked, and wondered with all my work, if there wasn't something else I could do? Was I doing my best?

There was every type of influenza: the gastric, meningeal, jaundiced and pneumonia. One poor boy had gotten well of pneumonia and still did not get better, but gradually worse. I was tending him one night when he put his head on my shoulder and said, "Sister, Sister, what is it? You have done your best; you have tried your hardest to pull me through, but I know I am going to die." He died that night and that is how it was all the time during that flu epidemic.

My officer in charge of my wards spoke to Matron. I think he saw that if I did not leave the ward, I, too, would soon become sick. So I was sent into the mess, away from the wards altogether, against my wishes. One of our sisters and officers died of the flu about this time.

When the flu abated somewhat, the General-in-Command used often to send an ambulance for the sisters to visit the various places of interest around. Brussels was one of the first cities we visited, reminding us very much of London, with its rush of traffic, wonderful shops and stately buildings. The Hotel de Ville was a wonderful building in the Grand Place, a big square surrounded by tall buildings with some wonderful architecture – turrets and different figures painted in gold. It seemed high in the heavens from the many surrounding buildings, making one glorious, golden sheen.

We went into the Hotel de Ville and were taken by an old French guide into the council room. This was an oblong room, with many fine mirrors and tapestries. The tapestries, we were told, were worth thousands of francs each. The guide pointed to the wonderful painted ceiling entitled 'The Meeting of the Gods', and made us understand, pointing to a figure with a huge trumpet, that he wanted us to walk, run and stand still in every part of the room and to watch the figure closely. We did so, and it did not matter which way you went or what position in the room you took, that figure was always pointing with its trumpet in your direction. One could almost see the figure move as we moved, it was most wonderful.

From here we were taken into the ballroom. Its walls were covered with fine paintings and hanging from its gloriously carved wooden ceiling were many wonderful flags and banners. The ballroom itself was very spacious with a fine floor. Leading from this room was a fine stone-paved hall, with a wide stone stairway and carved stone balustrade. Paintings and statues were everywhere and at the bottom of the stairway was the most beautiful bronze statue of St. Michel in armour, the wonderful bronze wings making a delightful picture against the white marble background. Lance and sword in hand, he stood on another male figure with wings. In the grounds, too, were some beautiful statues.

From the hotel we went to the cathedral, another magnificent building with more carvings inside. The King's Palace was not very far from here; also the museum, picture gallery and other places of interest, which we visited in turn. Then we took a trip to the lace-making part, each coming away with pieces of hand-made Brussels lace. Finally, we finished our day in a café, where we had tea and some of their lovely pastries. Then, boarding our ambulance, we were soon on our way to Namur, thoroughly tired out after our sightseeing day.

On three different occasions I was in Brussels and never tired of the city. There was always something fresh to see. One time we went round by the once beautiful city of Louvain, which now was lying mostly in ruins. The Germans had set fire to many of its fine buildings, as they had done in numerous towns. A great many of the people here were Dutch.

From Louvain, we went to famous Waterloo and saw many, many historical things. We saw the three monuments: the lion on its mound, forty-five metres high, with two hundred and twenty-six steps leading to the top. The lion was made by George Cockerill, from the guns taken by the Allies. We were told that the Belgian women carried the soil to make this mound, in buckets, for a centime a bucket. I climbed the two hundred and twenty-six steps, and on arriving at the top, after many rests on the way, was almost breathless; but the view of the surrounding countryside was worth it.

Then there was the monument to the Hanoverians – a truncated blue stone pyramid erected in 1818, and to the side of this, a monument dedicated to the memory of Sir Alexander Gordon, Knight-at-Arms of the Duke of Wellington, deadly wounded at the end of the battle. There was also the French monument, 'The Eagle Wounded to Death'. It was here that the last squares of the old guard stoically perished.

By the monument of the lion was the panoramic picture of the Battle of Waterloo. We spent quite a time here. The picture was so real we almost fancied we were watching the real battle; the great armies meeting, trampling over their dead and wounded, frantic horses, in many cases riderless, trampling over those already stricken down; guns in every direction, some spitting volumes of fire and smoke; others lying useless, the gunmen all killed or the guns broken to pieces. Headless, legless and armless men were lying everywhere – others, with swords pierced through their bodies, their eyes already glassy with death before they fell. We saw it all and it brought back to us the War we had just gone through, with the thought of the thousands and millions of boys dying the same way in the fight for freedom.

We visited Goumont or Hougoumont with the farm, chapel and well, all showing signs of heavy fighting. Bullet holes and splashes of darkened, aged blood were still to be seen. This was supposed to be one of the most interesting points in the battlefield on account of the important place it held during the battle and because it still bears traces of the struggle. The capture of this would have enabled Napoleon to outflank the allied armies. Mont-Saint-Jean Farm was used as a field hospital.

We also visited the farm of the Hais Sainte [La Haye Sainte: fought over throughout the day and defended by the King's German Legion.], captured by the French and retaken by the British, without fighting, at the end of the day. Finally going into the chapel, with its many memorial slabs in memory of English and Dutch officers who fell on that fateful day – 18th June, 1815. We finished our day shopping in Brussels and then returned to our billet in Namur.

Another time we had tickets given us to attend a concert given by the British Royal Engineer Band in the theatre at Brussels, a rotund building with its walls and ceilings of fresco paintings and many glittering lights. We had been seated some little time, with the bandsmen who were all in peacetime uniform, when the band suddenly commenced to play the Belgian National Anthem, 'La Brabançonne':

> *The days of slavery have vanished*
> *Now Belgium arise in thy might*
> *Your glorious past shall ne'er be banished*
> *Whilst thy sons for thee can fight.*
> *Emulate your heroes bold*
> *Strong in faith and valour be*
> *Thy motto thou must keep and hold*
> *Fight for King, the Law and Liberty*
> *Thy motto thou must ever keep and hold*
> *Fight for King, the Law and Liberty.*

Everyone immediately stood at attention and the officers at salute. Then we saw the King and Queen of Belgium and another lady entering a box, not twenty yards from where we were. The anthem finished, we all sat down and the concert commenced. It was a wonderfully selected programme and beautifully rendered.

At the close, the anthem was again played and then the people commenced to call, "Vive Le Roi, Vive Le Roi!" We saw the King hastily move his chair, beckon to the Queen to pick up her bouquet, which was lying on the ledge in front of the box, and quickly make their exit; not wishing to be detained by the crowd, we supposed. After a little supper, we prepared for our long journey home.

Things were still very quiet in the wards, just one or two sick cases coming in occasionally. This enabled us to continue with our 'joy rides'! One day about eight of us started for Dinant, a beautiful tourist resort on the banks of the River Meuse. We thoroughly enjoyed our drive, passing through some wonderful mountainous countryside. Dinant was lying three parts in ruins from fire and shell. The Germans had intended entire destruction of the town.

Six hundred and forty-seven civilians were killed in cold blood, either shot deliberately, burned to death or hung. There is a wall in one of the main streets from the Citadel which is absolutely riddled with bullet holes, with a bronze tablet bearing the inscription 'Martyrs of Liberty'. One hundred and sixteen men, women and children of all ages, some two months old, were shot down in cold blood on this spot. Even after they had fallen, the German soldiers still continued to fire into their already bullet-riddled bodies. Three hundred prisoners from the gaol were marched into the courtyard to be shot by the Germans, but the German soldiers took fright and panic reigned for some little time, saving those men's lives. But they were afterwards sent to Germany, where they were prisoners for three months. The panic was never accounted for.

A large workmen's apartment house, known as La Cité was set on fire. Locked in the burning building were the Michel family of four people, along with Georges A. Joinie. The screams of the unfortunate wretches condemned to the most horrible of deaths will ever ring in the ears of those who, hiding nearby, were compelled to listen. Buildings were set on fire, shots fired through windows, doors and cellars, killing and wounding many. Thirteen men were chained and marched to an orchard, where they were shot down in cold blood, while the German cavalrymen screamed, "Kill, kill. Hurrah, hurrah," in voices of demons, they say, rather than of men. Wives and children were compelled to witness the massacre of their own husbands and fathers.

We climbed the many steps (over four hundred) of the Citadel and were taken by a guide around the fort at the back of the Citadel. The east part is a comparatively level plateau. Here, in a cemetery made by the Germans, lie buried unknown English, French and Belgian soldiers, alongside their own. There is also a vault built in a dome shape, which contains German, Belgian, French and British soldiers. The Germans always kept the cemeteries in beautiful order. It was over this plateau that the Germans advanced from Liege and invaded the City of Dinant on August 15th, 1914, and at midday hoisted their flag at the Citadel.

As we looked around the devastated town and heard the different stories of the people, our hearts ached for them. Some of them were very bitter. We wondered how the Germans could have committed such atrocities in a town like Dinant, with such glorious scenery everywhere. They must have gone slightly mad; that seems to be the only solution.

From Dinant we went to Rochefort, as there were some wonderful caves we wanted to see; arriving there about four p.m. we got a guide from an *estaminet* in the village and were soon in the caves. After lighting lamps, he proceeded to take us down, down, down into the bowels of the earth. He told us these caves had been made by a volcanic eruption many years before.

Just as we got to the mouth of the cave, we heard a terrific rumble and had the guide not been with us and told us that this often happened, I think we would all have gone back. Through a narrow opening, with bent backs, we went, to find ourselves in a very spacious underground apartment. All kinds of structures had formed from the constant drip from the roof, such as chairs, etc., one being called 'the throne'. Another was shaped like a beautiful carved bed and deep down in the cave, down a narrow stone stairway, we heard a babbling brook and saw water, crystal clear, making its way with a merry gurgle of bubbles under some huge rocks. In another part of the cave a passage had been cut into the rocks by a huge body of water, which had managed to find its way out somewhere. The guide showed us different marks where the water had reached each year, until it had finally gotten away.

Even in this underground land, the Germans had had to destroy many of the best forms which attracted tourists to the spot, but the Belgian guide told us they had put in a claim for all the damages done. Only time will tell whether they get paid out or not.

In January, 1919, invitations were sent to as many of the sisters as would care to attend a Trooping of the Colours of the Bedfords and KOSB (Kings Own Scottish Border) Regiments, commemorating two hundred years ago that day when the Lincolns and Jocks fought side by side with the Dutch, and stormed the Citadel in Namur; also to commemorate the recent success of War when the Bedford and KOSB Regiments fought together.

The ceremony was to be held in the square in front of the Cathedral and when we got there, the troops were already in order. The KOSB were lining one half of the square and different streets leading to the square, with bayonets fixed; the Bedfords the other half and different streets in a like manner. In front of the Cathedral, in two lines, were arranged the Bedfords and the KOSB with their regimental bands, on either side – their officers standing in front; all with guns and bayonets fixed, awaiting the arrival of the General.

At one side of the square were two soldiers – one with fixed bayonet, the other with the colours covered, which the soldier with the bayonet was guarding. Very soon we heard a slight stir at the front of the square and noticed the arrival of the General. After a short speech telling us about the ceremony, the KOSB pipers' band marched across the square and were joined by the escort of the colours. They then proceeded to the side where the two solitary soldiers stood. The officer received the colours, unfurled them and amidst the pipers' playing, marched slowly, but impressively around the square, every man at the salute.

They were joined by the KOSB Regiment lined up in front of the Cathedral and then there was a grand march past of the troops. All eyes turned to the General as they passed him – the officers saluting. In a like manner followed the Bedfords and then with a loud rat, tat, tat of the drums, pipers' music and the Bedford Band they marched away, colours flying in the breeze. It was a very impressive sight and one I shall always remember.

Things continued very much the same. We were not kept very busy in the wards; mostly mild influenza cases. Sisters were constantly passing through Namur for the various CCS around, often staying one night at our hostel and continuing their journey on the morrow, by ambulance. We liked this, as those who had days off were able to go with them, returning with the ambulance in the evening. Another sister and myself were about to go off one day when orders came through for three sisters to proceed to Spa, so we asked if we might join them for the journey, and were allowed. It was at Spa that the Armistice was signed.

We were soon on our way along the banks of the River Meuse and about ten a.m. reached Huy, a very heavily fortified town, but very quaint with its narrow cobbled streets and picturesque buildings. From Huy we raced along to Liege, continuing our way on the river side. The scenery was glorious, with its many hills and dales and winding river.

Everywhere were signs of the army's victorious march to Germany. Flags and banners were flying and triumphal arches had been erected at intervals all along the route, bearing the inscription 'Welcome our Liberators'. We soon reached Liege and remained there for lunch, afterwards taking a look around the town. Liege is a large town with a very good shopping centre. After about an hour in Liege we proceeded on our way, crossing the river at one of its many bridges. We soon lost sight of that shimmering stream, arriving in Spa about two-thirty p.m. The CCS we were going to was situated some little distance from the town of Spa. However, we said our good-byes to the sisters and returned to Spa to sightsee.

Here, too, a great many of the finer buildings were lying in ruins where the Germans had set fire to them. We saw the hotel where the Armistice had been signed. The Germans still controlled this building and we saw a few of the German officers entering and leaving, but not in wartime uniform. They were in peace uniform. Some of them stared at us – others walked by as though we did not exist.

It was in Spa that the Kaiser was supposed to have had a wonderful dug-out, but we did not see this. About four o'clock we left Spa for Namur. Our driver took a short cut across country so we soon reached Huy, reaching Namur about nine p.m. Just as we got to the Bridge Jambres our car broke down, so we had to walk the rest of the way, sending on another ambulance to pick up our broken-down car.

In March I received a postcard from Captain Aylen, who had been promoted and transferred to Cologne, Germany. He said he had not heard from me in a long time; the next morning I received a letter from him which ought to have reached me a few weeks sooner. He told me of his journey to Germany and how he had tried to break his journey to see me. Evidently our letters had gone astray, so I immediately answered his letter. By this time we had become great friends and were trying to get leave together in England, but I was not able to manage it as there were so many due leave before me. On hearing this, Captain Aylen managed to get special French leave with permission to break his journey en route for Paris, at Namur and Tincourt, where we had met.

It was on 8th May, 1919, he came to Namur to spend a few days. Matron was very good and gave me my half-day and monthly day off, enabling me to be with him as much as possible. The afternoon of the 8th we strolled around the Citadel, taking many snaps of places of interest, arriving at the hostel in time for tea. After tea we played badminton in the grounds with two other sisters, thoroughly enjoying our game, giving us a great appetite for dinner, to which Captain Aylen stayed.

The next day we spent at Dinant. What a happy day it was. We both thoroughly enjoyed it and it was a red letter day for me, but I was feeling a little down-hearted at Captain Aylen's return to Germany on the morrow. That night I dined with him and then back to the hostel we came. The moon was shining brilliantly and the stars winked merrily at one another. The breeze stirred the trees to a gentle whisper and they told one another, perhaps, who knows, the same old story as was told to me under that spreading, blossoming hawthorn tree, its many white petals falling on our heads in the breeze, as though in blessing and forming a carpet at our feet.

When I got in that night I was met by one of the sisters, who informed me my orders were through for Charleroi, which meant rising early and packing. How I hated leaving Namur, which held such dear memories for me, and I did not like Charleroi. I had been told it was a smoky, dirty place, with almost two hundred coal mines surrounding the town. However, nothing could be done; I had to go and make the best of it.

The End in Sight: May 1919 – 26 October 1919

The ambulance arrived at the door about eleven a.m. and around one o'clock we entered Charleroi. I knew most of the sisters at 20 CCS, for which I was very thankful. I did not go on duty that day but unpacked and tidied my room, going on duty on the morrow to a ward of medical patients – about fifty in all. It was not long before I began to feel at home, but how I hated the place. It was the one spot in my overseas nursing that I disliked.

I soon heard from Germany that Captain Aylen was being demobilized and would be passing through Charleroi, where, for one fleeting hour, I would be able to see him before he went to England. The time soon passed and I looked forward to the hour I was to spend with him. It came on a Sunday and I rushed down to the station to find the train already in and 'my boy' waiting anxiously about. How the time flew. It seemed only a few minutes before that clock showed the hour had passed, a shrill whistle bringing everyone aboard and the train was soon rolling out of sight, leaving me very sad, standing on the platform.

It was not long before I found out that none of the sisters' leaves were due, so I decided to try for a 'special'. The sister in charge, in sympathy with me, helped me all she could and on June 2nd, 1919, I was taking that

Boulogne-Cologne express and was soon on the boat crossing the Channel, then to London, where I met 'my boy'. I got into mufti and we thoroughly enjoyed ourselves as the days raced along all too quickly, taking trips to our different people.

After a splendid holiday, I returned to France on 20th June, waiting at Boulogne until the ambulance train arrived for Charleroi. I arrived at Charleroi on 27th June and was immediately put on night duty in charge of prisoner-of-war wards. The day after my arrival, peace processions were being held by the Belgians and the British – both countries' soldiers taking part. Lorries were decorated in all kinds of fantastical pictures representing many different things. Most of the schoolchildren also took part in the procession.

Two touring cars were sent for the sisters, who had also been asked to take part. The colonel, sister in charge, another sister and I were in the first car with a driver, and there were four other sisters and a driver in the second car. We made a thorough tour of the town, amidst the many cries of the Belgian people, and finally finished in front of the Belgian Regimental Training School, where a Belgian regimental band was playing.

Time passed very quickly and it was not very long before I had news from America, telling me of the safe arrival of 'my boy'; and not very long before I received news to put in for demobilization.

We had many picnics these days, as there was very little work to do in the wards; and after peace was signed, all the sisters in the British Army were given a month in which to dance; a thing we had not been allowed to do since the War started. Parties were arranged at the different officers' mess, which we all attended; then the British Vice Consul of Charleroi entertained us several times with dances followed by supper.

On one of my days off, after coming off night duty, two of us sisters took the steamer and sailed down the canal to a beautiful little country spot called Abbaye d'Aulne and there, standing a little way from the waterside, was a big abbey lying in ruins. It looked as though it had been a most beautiful building, but had been wrecked in the Revolution many years before. Part of the building had been added to and was used for aged people as an almshouse. We spent the afternoon there, had tea at a nearby café and then walked along the canal side to a small town, where we took the electric streetcar back to Namur.

On September 10th, 1919, my demobilization came through and with all speed I packed, [*then*] caught the Boulogne Express; most of the sisters coming down to the station with me. Well I remember them too, making me sit on the carriage step so that they could in turn, rub shoulders with me. They said it was lucky to do so with anyone going off to get married and that it might bring the same good fortune to them. We laughed heartily and the train steamed out of the station amid a shower of rice, which one of the sisters had gotten from cook and put in her pocket, unbeknown to us.

How that train travelled, rolling from side to side. I really thought we could be derailed and how sick I became! I don't know which is worse, seasickness or train-sickness. They are both very unpleasant. Arriving in Boulogne the next morning, I reported at the hostel facing the station, and not feeling well, went straight to bed where I spent the entire day. The next morning, feeling better, I reported to our Principal Matron at Wimereux, where my final papers were signed. Matron thanked me for my services and wished me all happiness.

On 13th September, 1919, I sailed for England. Arriving at Folkestone, we were taken to the Dispersal Hostel, where we had to go through the last stages of demobilization. Another sister accompanied me who was also being demobilized. We stayed the night there. The matron in charge was a very sweet woman and did everything she could for us to get us away quickly.

More papers were signed and we were given an official dismissal from the army, which was worded thus:

CERTIFIED THAT STAFF NURSE B.H. HOPKINSON,
T.F.N.S. WAS DEMOBILIZED ON THE
14TH OF SEPTEMBER, 1919

Signed – G.S. Jacob, Matron,
Dispersal Hostel, Folkestone

We were also given a printed form of thanks, stamped with the British Coat of Arms, and worded thus:

IN SAYING GOOD-BYE TO
NO. L 69 RANK – STAFF NURSE
B.H. HOPKINSON
T.F.N.S. CORPS.
ON THE OCCASION OF HER DEMOBILIZATION, THE
GENERAL COMMANDING TROOPS, SHORNELIFFE, DESIRES

*TO PLACE ON RECORD, THE ARMY COUNCIL'S
APPRECIATION OF THE SERVICES RENDERED BY HER
DURING THE PRESENT WAR AND TO WISH HER ALL
SUCCESS AND PROSPERITY ON HER RETURN TO CIVIL LIFE.
HE TRUSTS THAT SHE WILL RETAIN THE KINDLIEST
FEELINGS TOWARDS HER OLD COMRADES OF ALL RANKS AND
TOWARDS THE UNITED UNITS IN WHICH SHE HAS SERVED.*

G.S. Jacob

This is a document we were all pleased to receive and something we shall always treasure.

We said good-bye to the Matron and were soon boarding the train en route for London. We arrived there about midday and I was able to take a taxi across London in time to catch a train for Nottingham, arriving there about six p.m.

Then started the work of getting my trousseau ready. This meant very hard work, as I had no civilian clothes at all. But with my sisters to help me, we were soon ready and on the 18th October, 1919, I sailed on the *Megantic* for Canada, arriving in Montreal on 26th October, after a very pleasant crossing. From Montreal, I took a two day journey to Winnipeg by train, where 'my boy' met me at the station.

* * *

ANNOUNCEMENT

*CAPTAIN C.H. AYLEN, R.A.M.C. OF PEMBINA, NORTH DAKOTA
AND
MISS BEATRICE H. HOPKINSON, OF NOTTINGHAM, ENGLAND,
FORMERLY OVERSEAS NURSE IN THE BRITISH ARMY,
WERE UNITED TOGETHER IN HOLY MATRIMONY
NOVEMBER FIRST, NINETEEN HUNDRED AND NINETEEN.
THE CEREMONY TAKING PLACE AT
DEVON COURT, WINNIPEG, CANADA.
THE REV. R.C. JOHNSTONE, LLD OFFICIATING
MANY FRIENDS AND RELATIVES OF THE GROOM WERE
PRESENT.*

Notes on the Diary Text

—∞—

1. Professional nurses were referred to as 'Sister' in order to differentiate them from the VADs, who were called 'Nurse'.

2. Charles Hopkinson was killed on 2 July 1916.

3. Mabel Whiffin.

4. Miss, subsequently Dame, Sidney Browne, herself a veteran of the Boer War.

5. This was the officers' hospital, where the nursing ratio would have been one nurse to six patients, as opposed to one to fourteen in the other ranks' wards.

6. Verey, or Very, lights were flares generally sent up over No-Man's Land to provide brief illumination for working parties.

7. Hazebroucke was a very important railhead and a key objective for the Germans.

8. The date is almost certainly wrong, as 47 CCS left Rosieres on 28 March 1918.

9. Staff from 32 CCS and 46CCS staff had evacuated ahead of 47.

10. It was not unusual for officers' hospitals to be at some distance from the main hospital or this may have been 41 Stationary which, like 42, was also in Amiens until 31 March 1918.

11. Two have been identified as Res Nurse I. Stambaugh USANC and Sister M. Patterson CAMC. As with all military awards at the time, sometimes it is hard to understand why one person received one and another not.

12. In fact she means 59GH.

13. For once Beatrice avoided severe bombing. The following night, 12 April, St Omer was once again under serious attack. 58 and 59GH were closed two days later.

14. On 14 April, just as Operation Georgette was starting.

15. Bergues, sometimes referred to as 'the other Bruges', suffered significant bomb damage in 1915.

16. The last line of German defences on the Western Front, 6,000 yards deep, ribbed with barbed wire and breached on 29 September, after four days' intensive fighting.

17. One was almost certainly Pte Henry Tandey VC, who also won the DCM and the MM in September 1918.

18. In fact, Villers-Bretonneux was the scene of exceptionally fierce fighting in April 1918 and was captured by the Australians on 25 April. It was also where the first tank-on-tank battle took place.

19. Pseudonym of the Australian poet J.M. Harkin.

20. There were extensive luggage facilities for nurses at Boulogne, much of it supplied by the Hotel Louvre.

21. There had been considerable difficulties relating to transporting sisters to CCS in this area and Maud McCarthy appears to have been instrumental in arranging for them to be taken on Ambulance Trains.

22. About 285 kms from Wimereux.

23. Beatrice's information here is incorrect. The Germans did not have a Women's Auxiliary Army Corps. The WAAC was the British Corps, formed in 1917, and they were never stationed in Namur.

Appendix I

Wartime Letter
by Dr Charles H. Aylen
April 1918

—⚋⚋—

This letter was written from a farm house in France, on 27 April 1918, by Charles Aylen to his friend Mr Thompson in Pembina, North Dakota. Upon the death of Dr Aylen's mother, the letter was found in her papers.

A Farm House, France
April 27th, 1918

Dear Mr. Thompson,

When things are quiet here, as they are just now, I usually take advantage of it by writing a line or two to someone back home. I am just thinking of what a delightful time I will have when everyone I have written to answers their letters. So [far] I have received no mail at all from anyone at home, but I am expecting to receive some at any time now, and you may be sure we appreciate letters out here.

Since writing, Mr. Thompson, just before leaving England, I have seen and been through a few things which I thought you might like to hear about and which would give you some idea of the work we do as Battalion Medical Officers.

When I last wrote I was under orders for Italy, in fact I was on embarkation leave, when the Boche started his big push towards Amiens.

Those orders were immediately cancelled and I was sent over to France at once. We had a delightful trip across the Channel on Sunday, March 24th, despite the fact that everything was done in such a hurry.

[*Censored section*] A Boche plane was over the city observing the damage they had done the previous night in an air raid. It was our first initiation into warfare and it was quite exciting to watch the anti-aircraft guns or Archies as they are called, trying to hit him; he managed to get away tho'.

I spent two days at a base hospital near Boulogne and then drove from there to Namps, a distance of about ninety miles, by ambulance, over magnificent roads and thru [*sic*] a most beautiful country; hills and valleys all the way. The whole of the distance we passed groups of French refugees and British transport of all descriptions, guns, ammunition and men being rushed to stop the German rush.

That evening after dark we went thru the city, which was the German objective. I shall never forget it. It is a large place, about eighty thousand, and considered a fine place. It was like a huge vaulted cemetery, not a light was to be seen and the streets were absolutely deserted. The people having fled. As we left the place, we passed hundreds of people on the road, hurrying to get away; some almost too old to walk and others almost too young, and to add to their misery it was raining very heavily. I thought when I saw them, if all our people back home could see the misery of these poor unfortunates, they would soon put an end to all the rotten Pro-Germanism and meddling pacifism which is eternally showing itself.

For a week I was attached to a field ambulance and enjoyed it very much. The Colonel commanding and all the other officers were very fine men and as we were back in a quiet area, it was very pleasant. Just at this time, however, the Boche started another push up North against the Portuguese, our illustrious ally, as the papers put it, who appear to know a damn sight more about running than they do about fighting! [*The Portugese had entered the war in March 1916.*] At any rate, they went thru them like greased lightning and it wasn't until they pulled them out of the line and put in a couple of British regiments that they checked his push.

I was attached as Medical Officer to one of the Battalions that was to take over the line. Their previous MO, who was also an American, had either been killed or captured a short time before. We had to march ten miles through the rain; it always rains over here when there is a march to make, and took the train, all cattle cars which say on them 8 *chevaux* or 40 *hommes,* meaning 8 horses or 40 men.

We rode north all night and all the next day, about ten miles per hour. I am sure the man who wrote 'On a Slow Train Thru [*sic*] Arkansas' must have gotten his inspiration from that particular train! At last about 5 p.m. we detrained and had tea. The British Army simply could not fight without its afternoon tea. We have it every day at 4.30 p.m. within 1000 yards of the front line trenches.

We then started on another ten-mile jaunt. Fortunately, however, my horse was there so I rode. We were to stop at a small village where we expected to remain all night, but had only been there about two hours when the Colonel came along and said that we were to take up the position at once. The Battalion immediately fell in and started off on another march of several miles to get the position of the trenches located, which is no easy task in a strange place and it was a very dark night. At last, just an hour or so before dawn, the places were found and the men immediately got busy to dig themselves in, for as soon as it got light the Boche would be popping machine gun bullets at them. I then went with the head-quarters staff about a mile to the left and established a dressing station.

All morning things were comparatively quiet, but along toward noon the Boche brought up a number of machine guns and things began to get warmer. Just after lunch a chap came running up to the post and asked me to go with him across a field to see a soldier who was shot thru the lung. Just when we got there, they turned a machine gun on us and believe me I put in a warm few minutes until we got the chap in.

The rest of the day, they simply plastered that house with bullets; they were continually coming thru the door and windows. A Major with us had one put thru a tin cup hanging on his belt. Luckily the house was brick or it would have been untenable. A little later they got guns on both sides of us and then we did have to look sharp. My stretcher bearers had to walk thru a mile of that all afternoon. There wasn't one of them that didn't deserve a V.C. that day. Shooting at stretcher bearers and Red Cross ambulances seems to be the Huns' favourite pastime. I didn't use to believe all the yarns we heard and read about these pet tricks of the Boche, but believe me, I know now that they were true.

About five that evening, they started to strafe us with some fairly heavy high explosive shells, so we decided to shift quarters. We moved a mile back and had a very pleasant trip to the music of more machine gun bullets. We hadn't left the house long when he put three shells into it in quick succession. Lucky for us we weren't there.

That night it was very quiet, for which we were thankful, as it enabled us to get some much required sleep; we had had none for the previous three days.

We were now located at the edge of a small village and the first thing in the morning Fritzie began to warm things up with his high explosives. He everlastingly pasted that village for about an hour and then started throwing them over our way and, I assure you, that about that time I was wishing I was back in the U.S.A. I had just run across the road to speak to the adjutant and was coming out of his door when a shell came thru the roof of my ain [*own*] post, killing one man outright, desperately wounding another and more or less injuring a number of others.

By the time I got to him, the wounded chap had crawled out in front of the building and whilst we were dressing him, two more shells hit the building. How, in thunder, we managed to escape injury is beyond me. However, I have a beautiful dent in my steel helmet as a souvenir of the occasion.

Again we had to vacate hurriedly and also again he dropped three shells into headquarters shortly after we left. This time we moved into a deserted farmhouse; a very well-constructed brick house, with an excellent cellar which afforded us good protection when the shelling got too heavy. We were able to stay here in comparative comfort the remaining time we were in the line.

He used to shell us regularly three times every day and usually once in the night. One shell exploded just outside my windows and put two pieces thru the windows and across the room just above the bed where I was sleeping, another came thru the wall; not exactly conducive to sound sleep, but you can bet that I keep pretty close to the floor!

We were in the line a week that time and then were sent back about two miles to a small village for a forty-eight hour rest. I have had some rests but never, I hope, one like that again. For fully an hour before we started back, which of course is always after dark, it had been absolutely quiet; not a gun fired, which was very unusual. I was with a party of about 150 men, and we had gone about half way when the Boche opened up a terrific barrage.

To describe heavy shell fire, or one's sensations while under it, is absolutely impossible; one simply had to experience it. There have been times in my life when I have been mortally afraid, but never was I ever so positively petrified with fear as that night. The screech of the shells is simply hellish and their detonation terrific. The air was simply alive with them; our only protection was to drop flat. If we could only have seen it wouldn't have seemed so bad, but we were going across fields and the country here is full of ditches with water in them, so we had to go very slowly. For an hour and a half we were in it and I am sure if it had lasted another half hour I should have turned grey. The next afternoon I walked back over the same ground. I shall never understand how we ever managed to get there. The whole place we came thru was a mass of shell holes.

We all became fatalists. After a few such experiences, it is the only view that we can take with any comfort. If a shell has your name on it, you're done for; is about the way we look at it. There is only one redeeming feature I know of to shell fire, and that is, that the shell that hits one, he never hears. The only shells you hear are the ones that pass above or to the side of you and you just have time to fall flat and get a measure of protection.

The speed of these shells is so terrific that they travel faster than the sound. I have seen shells exploding half a mile beyond me before I heard the screech of them. The remainder of that night we were fairly quiet, but the next night, while still at rest, he again shelled us for over two hours and gave us six casualties. So, our rest for that night was gone.

The next night we moved up in line again, a little to the right of where we had been before... Just here I made a hurried exit to the cellar. He started to shell us pretty vigorously and when he blew out a window within two feet of me, I thought it about time to retire.

To continue … and I established my aid post in another deserted farm house; a fine old place with a great many trees about and a good size orchard. The apple trees are in bloom right now and it was fine to get out for a walk when things were quiet.

One evening, just at sunset, after a beautiful day, I was out for a walk and counted forty of our planes coming back from a raid on the Hun lines. They came in relays of fives and tens and flying like flocks of geese. There were huge bombing planes and the little fast scouts kept continually circling the larger bombers like destroyers about a battle ship. We very seldom see a Boche plane over our lines at this point and [when] one does get up enough nerve to come over, he is very soon chased off.

Those four days in the line were very quiet and we were not badly shelled once, except one night he threw over a lot of gas shells which caused me to wake up sneezing and rubbing my eyes. We again went back to our rest camp for another forty-eight hours and this time we were fairly quiet.

We then moved position and came into the same line as the night before last; we alternate between the two. Again we had to walk thru heavy shelling. Just before I reached the building a shell exploded in the courtyard; it killed ten men and two mules attached to a limber; seriously wounding twelve others. The boy who was holding the mules was the closest to the shell, but was the least hurt of all. One man's legs and head were completely blown off.

It is the artillery that is making this war the hell that it is. A man can face machine gun fire, even tho' the whine of the bullet is not the most pleasant thing in the world; but man was never expected to face shell fire; it is too hellish and its destructive force is too great. I know of nothing worse than to see a man struck by a shell and shattered beyond all resemblance to a human being. It is that, that shatters a man's nerves and makes doddering idiots of so many who have been subjected to it for long periods.

The regular British Tommy is a remarkable character. As a soldier he is absolutely unbeatable, because he never knows when he is beaten. It is a lucky thing for us that the German staff haven't got the British Tommies for their soldiers, because I think a combination of the two would be almost unbeatable. We certainly have to give them credit for having a mighty efficient general staff.

We are all hoping it will be over soon, but I can see no reason why it should stop for a long time to come. What conditions are like in Germany, we can only surmise. We hardly ever see a paper out here, and then, only an old one. The Boche prisoners tell us they are weary of it all and many of them are only too glad to be taken prisoners. Many of them are mere boys, but others are prime young men and fully confident of victory.

Anyone who is foolish enough to believe that the morale of the German Army is broken and that they can be easily beaten is only deluding himself and is living in a fool's paradise. The sooner the people at home, in all the Allied countries, come to a full realization of what this

War is, the same as the French people have, and stop their childish prattle and produce more concrete facts, the better it will be for them.

We have deluded ourselves about long enough with the economic conditions in Germany. I fail to see where conditions in Germany have any bearing on the case whatsoever, so long as their army remains the fighting force that it is. We go along from day to day telling ourselves that the German people have about reached the limit of their endurance, and in the meantime they throw a million fresh troops into this front and win a few more victories.

When England, Canada and the United States get down to brass tacks and stop their pussyfooting with Ireland, the French Canadian in Quebec and the Pro-Germans and Pacifists, and throw every ounce of their energy into it, then, and not until then, are we going to see the finish of it all. Five million American troops is what we want over here; nothing less.

Everyone over here is expecting great things of the American boys and I am sure that they will fully live up to that expectation. I am inclined to think that the ingenuity of the Yankee boys will have the tendency to get Fritzie's goat or get his wind up, as they say over here. For if there is one thing he doesn't like, it is to have new stunts pulled off on him.

There is no doubt that a great many old, foolish, prejudices between the American and English people will be wiped out and bring a closer co-operation between the two, which is most certainly to be desired.

One sees almost as many American doctors attached to British regiments now as British doctors. Most of them were sent over when the U.S. first declared war, to take training in England and have since been attached to various regiments. There were fifty of them came to France the same day I did. I have talked to a great many of them and they were all very well satisfied with being attached to British regiments.

Our rationing is amazingly good. We always have plenty of everything; plenty of butter, eggs and milk and always meat three times every day; and as I said before, we always have tea at 4.30 p.m. war or no war!

I am anxious to hear about Vernon, and sincerely trust he is coming thru everything safely. I am sure we will have a few things to tell one another when we get home.

A Fritz plane just came over quite low, to observe and usually after such a stunt we get a good shelling; so I expect to repair cellar-wards before long.

If by any chance you should see any of my people, do not tell them any of these things I have spoken of, as the less they know the less they have to worry about. Most people imagine that a medical officer gets a wonderful experience with absolutely no danger to himself. So, if that is their belief, so much the better.

Remember me to all. Tell Neeta to be sure to write.

Very sincerely,

Charlie

Appendix II

An Account Written by Dr Charles H. Aylen on Armistice Day, 22 November 1922

—ᴍ—

Today, our minds, with one accord, go back to that bleak November morning in 1918, when the whole world was thrilled by the signing of an armistice, bringing to a close the greatest war in which the powers of this world had ever engaged. It is with a deep emotion that we commemorate this day, and in commemorating it, pay homage to those men and women who, like the Crusaders of old, died fighting for their God and Country. It is fitting and proper that we should do this.

In the year 1776, there was fired in America a shot which was heard round the world. It was the beginning of a struggle which was to end once and for all, an unbearable tyranny and oppression, and out of which was destined to grow a nation which one day was to take her place in the very front rank of great nations.

This was not the first or only shot heard round the world. Through the ages, each nation, as she rose from despotism, had done so by the blood of her patriots. And so, on that fateful June 28th, 1914, in Sarajevo, Serbia, another shot was heard round the world.

Little did we, following our peaceful avocations, realize that in a short time the shot fired by little Serbia, against the oppressor Austria, would draw us into a frightful maelstrom of war. Little, too, did we realize that there ruled in Germany a man, strutting about in his own pompous vainglory and egotism, who talked of treaties as scraps of paper, of military necessity knowing no law, of might making right, sinking the ships of neutral nations without a trace, of ruling the world and his place in the sun, until, as Victor Hugo said of Napoleon, "God was bored by him".

What is this thing called war? Is it the marching of a battalion behind a playing band? Is it the waving of flags and cheering? Is it the last frantic goodbye as the train bears the loved one away? No, – none of these. Gilbert Frankau, in a poem [*'The Other Side'*] has told us what war really is [Here Charles quotes the full poem].

God forbid that on this day our thoughts should be narrow and confined to the memory of our own Nation's dead alone, glorious as that memory may be. Let us keep sacred in our memories those glorious Australians and New Zealanders fighting to their last breath at Gallipoli, martyrs to a useless sacrifice. But what a sacrifice.

And shall we not pause with reverence as we think of those inspired French troops before Verdun. 'They shall not pass', we hear them say, and to the end of the world that noble sacrifice will be a heritage to us all.

What of those thousands of pitiful wooden crosses which mark the resting place of England's dead? Think of those fifty thousand lives in the very prime of manhood snuffed out in a single day at that terrible Battle of Loos. Hemmed in by enemy machine gunners, refusing to retreat, but inch by inch going doggedly onward. Truly the spirit of Nelson was with those troops that day. Again, perhaps a useless sacrifice. But what a sacrifice.

And those noble Canadian boys at Ypres, when that fearful cloud of choking poison gas came upon them. Let us remember in deepest gratitude, how they held the line whilst others ran screaming from the field.

While we today think of our own boys lying over there, let us think for just a moment of those other mothers' sons. Let us think of them today, as 'only our boys':

Lord God of Hosts,
Be with us yet,
Lest we forget,
Lest we forget.

It is right that we should think of them today, but let it not be the remembrance of pity, rather let it be the proud remembrance of work well done. They fought like men. They died like men. Let us remember them in the words of Byron [in the play *Marino Faliero*, about a fourteenth century Doge of Venice.]:

> *They never fail who die in a great cause...*
> *Though years elapse, and others share as dark a doom,*
> *They but augment the deep and sweeping thoughts,*
> *That overpower all others, and conduct the world at last to freedom.*

Appendix III

'A Mother's Prayer'
by Beatrice Aylen

—ᴍᴍ—

This poem was written when Beatrice's three sons were heading off to serve in World War Two. All three returned safely.

Dear God, how shall I pray
For these, my sons, who have gone away.
Shall I pray them safe return,
To home, and hearts that ache and yearn
Or shall I pray, they to carry on
This fear to overcome.

Shall I pray that they may live
Whilst other sons, their lives may give?
No dear Lord; I shall pray though steep
and rugged lie the way,

That thou might always be their guide
And give them faith – steadfast and high
And hope like ours to light their way,
Strengthened courage to obey
Whatever comes along the way

And when at last they may return
If sick and maimed, then give me strength
to carry on their courage to return,
Help me God, new hope to give
These sons of mine so they may live.

Editor's Note: In the Great War, it was very common for women as well as men to express their thoughts, hopes and fears through the medium of poetry. Although poetry was a less popular genre in the Second World War, a substantial amount was written. What cannot easily be said in prose can frequently be expressed in verse.

Beatrice quotes several poets in her memoir, showing that she was familiar with and indeed comfortable with the genre. In addition, her education in the late 1890s would have introduced her to many of the great English poets. It is unsurprising that when her emotions were so deeply roused, when her own sons went off to war – and she knew better than many mothers what they might face – that she seeks to explore her feelings in verse.

Index